JOHN DAWSO

SAINT JOHN
5792
EXPIRATIO
11 NOV 1989
8 NOV 1989
For the purpose of
IMMIGRATION SERVICE
1 2 MAR 1992
DEPARTED
(2212)
HONG KONG
IMMIGRATION SERVICE
10 MAR 1992
DEPARTED
(3195)
HONG KONG
Permitted to remain
1 0 JUN 1992
Visitor Permitted to remain
until
8 JUN 1992
-8 MAR 1992
HONG KONG
IMMIGRATION SERVICE
10 MAR 1992
(3172)
HONG KONG
1 JAN 2002
УКРАЇНА
Бориспіль
FIJI
1 4 APR 1997
DEPARTED
IMMIGRATION
36 ARRIVAL
14 FEB 1996
MALTA IMMIGRATION
36
IMMIGRATION FIJI
FOR FOUR MONTHS
0 9 APR 1997
SRI LANKA
IMMIGRATION
20 NOV
Canada

John Dawson
Lifebook

First published by John Dawson in 2024
Dublin, Ireland
Email: dawson@iol.ie
Text © John Dawson

The right of John Dawson to be identified as the author of this work has been asserted by him.

All rights reserved. No part of this publication maybe be reproduced in any form or by any means without the prior permission of the publisher.

Every effort has been made to trace or contact all copyright holders. The publisher will be pleased to make good any omissions or rectify any mistakes brought to their attention at the earliest opportunity.

In My Life

There are places I'll remember
All my life, though some have changed
Some forever, not for better
Some have gone and some remain

All these places had their moments
With lovers and friends, I still can recall
Some are dead and some are living
In my life, I've loved them all

Lyrics by John Lennon and Paul McCartney

FOREWORD BY PAT RABBITTE

In the era of fake news and conspiracy theories, this memoir is likely to give rise to questions in some quarters as to whether the John Dawson we all know and love is a more mysterious figure than we all thought. Could a man who has more frequently criss-crossed the globe than John Le Carré – sometimes to the most unlikely and obscure places – have avoided the odd clandestine contract for the CIA? Or maybe he was just fascinated by the aviation sector.

There is no doubt about the latter. From an early age our hero found everything to do with aeroplanes absorbing. Using his old passports, starting in 1969, he has constructed a roadmap that enables him to summon up memories of places and people. A good memory and his customary boundless enthusiasm have come together to produce a most enjoyable narrative.

Born in London to an English baptist father and Irish Catholic mother, reared and schooled in Dublin, the young Dawson was an energetic rugby scrum half without ever threatening to displace any of Jamison Gibson-Park's predecessors. He also dabbled in music forming a small rock n' roll band even if the name – The Nuts – failed to presage the creativity of the future marketing consultant.

The author cut his teeth with the student travel company USIT, which for years despatched some 10,000 students on temporary work visas to the United States on charter flights. This innovative programme first devised by USIT founder the late Gordon Colleary put more students at the time, myself included, through higher education than the Irish government.

Of course, John had done the usual summer jobs but the one that intrigues me is when he stood in as cook – chef would be a bit grandiose – on a research trawler, Cú na Mara, out of Kinsale!

Having married Jackie at 23, he took the big step of becoming a travel or tourism consultant where his easy facility for networking served him well. His work with former Soviet Bloc countries is well remembered, but given recent events, none is more interesting or funny than his long association with Ukraine, where he was initially recruited on behalf of Guinness Peat Aviation as part of a team of industry experts to manage the setting up of a new airline.

None of the many projects, some in fairly primitive and inauspicious circumstances, that he was concerned with are as intriguing for the Irish reader as his account of being in at the origins of Ryanair. The descriptive narrative of the build-up to, and preparation for, the inaugural flight on May 23rd 1986 is riveting. I do not recall this type of insight and first-hand evidence featuring in anything I have read before about the new airline.

From Hong Kong to Havana (where the author was sunburned while listening to a short two-hour speech by Fidel Castro), from Beijing to Bangkok and from Zambia to Oman the writer demonstrates a memory like the elephant that he claims walked past his grandmother's house in Cavan when he was a boy to advertise the circus coming to town. There is no end to those passport stamps and that's before we get onto the Falklands Islands, the Dutch Windward Islands and the capitals of an array of other islands where I didn't even know there were islands.

A life well lived.

Pat Rabbitte served as Minister for Communications, Energy and Natural Resources from 2011 to 2014, leader of the Labour Party from 2002 to 2007 and a Minister of State from 1994 to 1997. He is currently Chairman of TUSLA, the Child and Family Agency.

ACKNOWLEDGEMENTS

I could never have persevered with this project without the support and encouragement of my family and friends. I've been blessed to have known and worked with wonderful people in Ireland and around the world.

A special thanks to Liz Meldon and my daughter Amy for proof reading and encouragement; Des Kiely for his design and production advice; Robert Doran for doing the editing and to Jackie for indulging me during this project. Last but not least I'd like to thank Pat Rabbitte for writing such a witty and inciteful foreword.

PREFACE

I recently rediscovered my first passport, and as I flicked through the pages, the various official stamps and visas brought back memories of the places I'd been, people I'd met, and things I'd done in my first thirty-odd years in the travel industry.

My first passport was issued on 4 September 1969 and, together with the subsequent five, gave me a record of my travels recorded by nameless immigration officers around the world as entry and exit stamps.

I've spent a fair amount of time on my own in hotel rooms around the world, and I thought that the downtime would be a good opportunity to chronicle some of my experiences. We live in changing times, and while every generation claims to have seen unprecedented change, I feel the period between 1969 and 2022 has brought more than its fair share of technological, cultural and social changes.

I consider myself a lucky person who has benefited from more than my share of serendipity and being in the right place at the right time. Despite having failed in the world of academia, I found a career niche as an aviation and tourism consultant. I made a modest living, paid my bills, and never had a bad debt in over thirty years of being self-employed.

My primary motivation for writing this 'lifebook' is to give my grandchildren and those that follow an insight into my life, my times and their heritage.

A few of the following stories have been romanticised, and the keen-eyed reader may take issue with some of my dates and facts, but as Mark Twain said, 'Never let the truth get in the way of a good story.'

Things I wish I'd asked
For myriad reasons and circumstances, I know precious little about my parents' early life, how and when they met, their wartime experiences and their first couple of years in Ireland. Family and personal events were more difficult to catalogue (and recall), because for most of my life there were no selfies or such to act as aide-mémoires.

As an only child I was lucky and privileged to be raised by two wonderful parents who instilled me a belief in the importance of tolerance, courtesy, honesty and kindness. My father was raised a Baptist, but I don't remember him going to church; my mother was a practising Roman Catholic, and I went to Mass with her in Kilmacud parish church. I made my first Holy Communion and Confirmation, and while I've never been a practising Catholic, I try and practise core Christian values.

I wish I'd asked my parents more questions and that they had been around to share some of the joyous moments of my adult life. I miss them still.

LE BOURGET
4 SEP 1975
FRANCE
48
CUSTOMS
IMMIGRATION
DOUANES
IMMIGRATION
SEP 27 1980
TORONTO
30 OCT 1976
HEATHROW (2)
-9 JUL 1985
IRELAND
(49)
23 APR 1983
GATWICK
FRANCE
A 278
DAR-EL-BEIDA
CANADA
ORT ERIE
IMMIGRATION OFFICER
19 OCT 1983
MAIQUETIA-088
DIEX
19 FEB. 1982
SALIDA
VENEZUELA
GUARDA FISCAL
SERV FRONTEIRAS

CONTENTS

Foreword by Pat Rabbitte		6
Preface		9

PART I

Chapter 1	Early Years	15
Chapter 2	Growing Up	20
Chapter 3	Early Home Life	24
Chapter 4	Hobbies and Influences	29
Chapter 5	Coming of Age	33
Chapter 6	Rugby in My Life	36
Chapter 7	USIT Years	42
Chapter 8	Ryanair	47
Chapter 9	Becoming a Consultant	55
Chapter 10	Treasured Traditions	58

PART II

Chapter 11	Bitten by the Travel Bug	63
Chapter 12	All at Sea, 1967	65
Chapter 13	First Flight, 1968	67
Chapter 14	America, 1970	69
Chapter 15	Summer in New York, 1974	76
Chapter 16	Bangkok Quickie, 1976	79
Chapter 17	Viva Cuba, 1978	84
Chapter 18	Flying on Concorde, 1983	89
Chapter 19	Aruba, 1990	92
Chapter 20	Italia 90	93

Chapter 21	LOT Polish Airlines, 1991	98
Chapter 22	African Flying Boat, 1992	100
Chapter 23	Ukraine International Airlines, 1992	103
Chapter 24	Romania, 1993	109
Chapter 25	Dutch Windward Islands, 1994	111
Chapter 26	Aviaprima Sochi, 1994	112
Chapter 27	Eritrea, 1994	115
Chapter 28	Canada, 1995	118
Chapter 29	Colombia, 1995	121
Chapter 30	Armenia, 1996	123
Chapter 31	Falkland Islands, 1997	126
Chapter 32	Tuvalu, 1997	130
Chapter 33	Coast Starlight: California, 1997	136
Chapter 34	Kaliningrad, 1998	139
Chapter 35	Pacific Odyssey, 1998	141
Chapter 36	South Africa, 1998	144
Chapter 37	Pakistan, 1998	146
Chapter 38	Oman, 2003/4	148
Chapter 39	Moldova, 2004	155
Chapter 40	Iran, 2004	156
Chapter 41	Zambezi Airlines, Zambia, 2008	158
Chapter 42	Montserrat, 2009	162
Chapter 43	Proflight Zambia, 2010	166
Chapter 44	Mozambique, 2012	168
Chapter 45	Kenya, 2014	170
Chapter 46	Sardinia, 2014	174
Chapter 47	Madeira, 2020	178

PART I

CHAPTER 1

Early Years

Beginnings

I was born in Mile End Road hospital in the Eastend of London on 20 February 1950; the hospital is within the sound of Bow Bells, so technically I'm a Cockney. My mother was Maureen Caffrey, originally from Drumalee, just outside Cavan town, and my father was Clifford (Cliff) Dawson. He was from Colchester, an old Roman town in Essex.

I don't know much about my parents' early life together, such as how and where they met. But I do know that

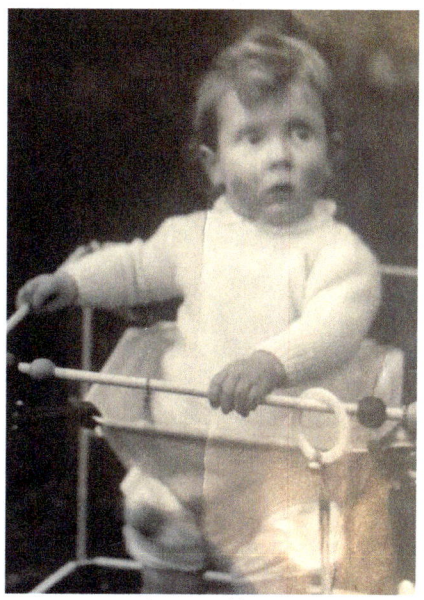

One year old me.

my mother did her nursing training in England, and from 1936 to 1939 she was based in Plaistow Fever Hospital and there is a record of her working in Newton Abbot General Hospital in December 1948. Unfortunately there are no records of the missing years. My father was a hospital lab technician, working and living in Colchester.

Wartime

At the outbreak of World War II, my father joined the Royal Observer Corps, whose members were predominately part-time volunteers. He would have been equipped with high-powered binoculars and responsible for identifying and reporting German aircraft approaching the east coast of England.

When I was younger, I used to hear stories that my mother was a nurse in a 'fever hospital' in the East End of London during the Blitz, which I now believe was Plaistow Fever Hospital, as mentioned above.

William J Dawson
1897-1990

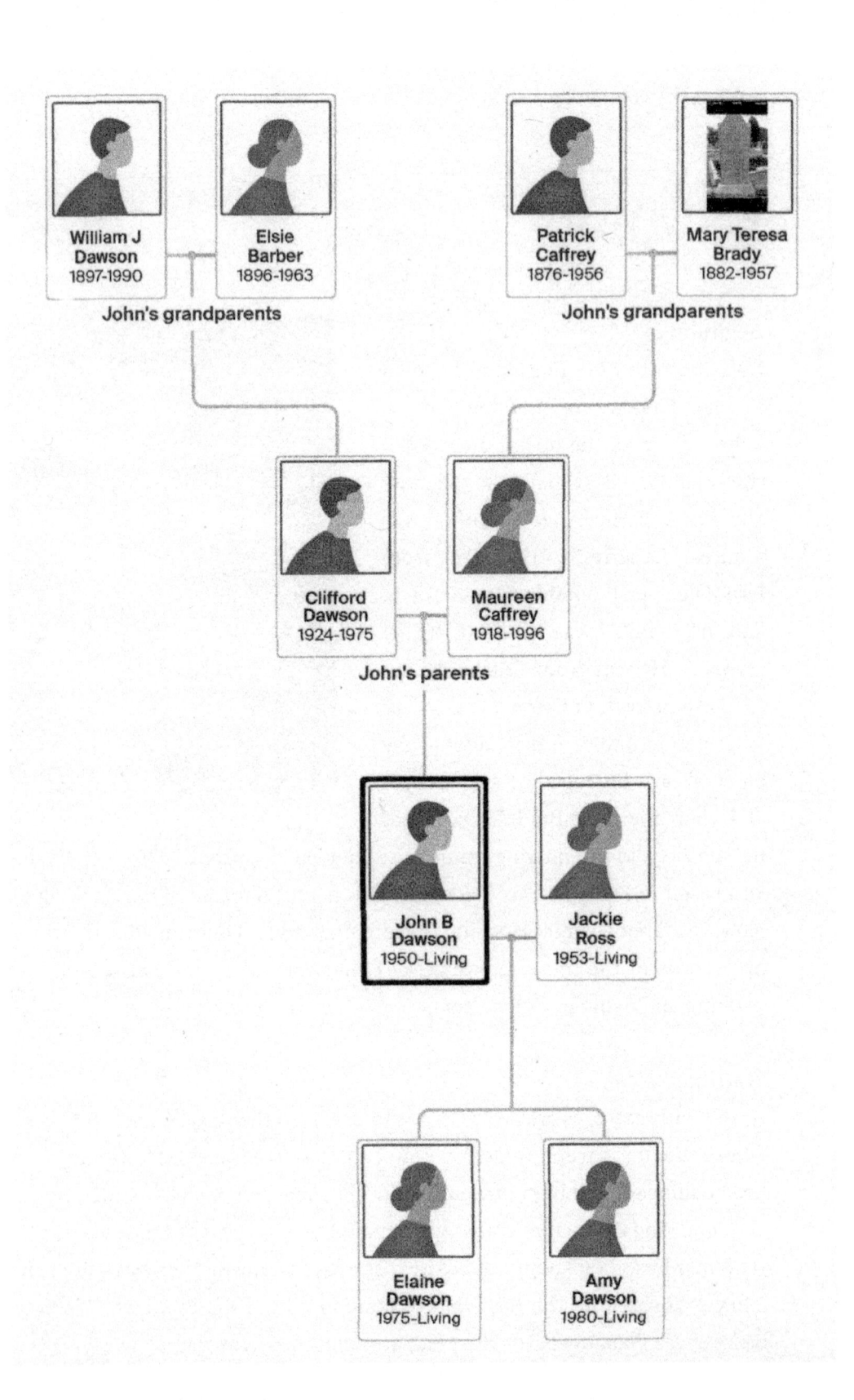

Elsie Barber
1896-1963

John's grandparents

Patrick Caffrey
1876-1956

Mary Teresa Brady
1882-1957

John's grandparents

Clifford Dawson
1924-1975

Maureen Caffrey
1918-1996

John's parents

John B Dawson
1950-Living

Jackie Ross
1953-Living

Elaine Dawson
1975-Living

Amy Dawson
1980-Living

I only wish I'd been more inquisitive and found out more about her wartime experiences, but her generation were reluctant to speak about the war years.

Post-war

My parents were married in Colchester in September 1945, and they lived in a rented cottage in a village called Stanway on the outskirts of Colchester. Around that time they acquired a beautiful collie named Biddy, who would eventually move with them to Ireland. To remind her of home, my mother named the house in Stanway Cavan Cottage. Stanway is now part of suburban Colchester but recently I managed to pin-point the location of their old house and I contacted the present owners. They very kindly sent me a contemporary photo of the house, and I was delighted to see a familiar sign on the gate, even if Cavan was misspelled.

In Britain, food rationing continued into the mid-fifties, and to stretch the meagre rations my mother kept both rabbits and hens.

In the 1950s airfares were high, and boat and train journeys were arduous. Leisure travel as we know it didn't exist. My father rarely visited his parents or sister, Mary, but his father came to Ireland in 1962 and we brought him on holidays to the Dingle Peninsula in County Kerry, where he painted some lovely seascapes, one of which I inherited.

My English heritage

My grandfather, William Dawson, was born in 1897. He worked for the local council and lived just outside Colchester, where he died in 1990. He was an accomplished amateur artist and I have several of his paintings at home.

I credit Grandfather Dawson with nurturing my artistic side, which has trickled down to my daughters and their children. I have only scant memories of my grandmother, Elsie, who died in 1963.

I wasn't particularity close to my English cousins, Mark and Andrew, but we'd meet up when I occasionally went to Colchester to visit my Aunt Mary.

My Irish heritage

The Caffrey family home was at the crossroads in Drumalee, a townland just outside Cavan town on the road to Cootehill. My grandfather built his own modest wooden house, which was eventually demolished, and my Uncle Paul built a bungalow on the site. Some years later my cousin Padraic built a new family home on the same site, which he lives in to this day. My cousin Paul lives in Waterford, and my youngest cousin, Aidan, lives in Virginia, County Cavan. I had another cousin, Lawrence, who sadly died in a car crash in 1988.

My parents and I regularly visited my maternal grandparents, Patrick and Mary Caffrey, in Cavan. Before we owned a car, my father would either borrow or hire one for the trip. As a twelve-year-old boy I'd be sent out to fetch a bucket of water from a nearby well because, at the time, my grandparents' house had no running water. There was no bathroom – I'd have a bath sitting in a tin bath filled with saucepans of hot water from the range in the kitchen.

My parents with Biddie outside Cavan Cottage in Colchester.

My grandfather had a small field where he'd cut grass with a scythe to make hay. It was a long process: the hay would be left to dry and then turned and eventually stacked into stooks and left to dry out completely. Towards the end of the summer, the stacks would be winched up onto a horse-drawn cart and brought to the barn next to my grandparents' house. I was allowed sit up on the cart as we clip-clopped the couple of miles home.

One incident stands out in my memory. We'd driven from Dublin, and my grandparents were in the yard to greet us. I had only just got out of the car when their Kerry Blue dog jumped up a bit me on the arm. My grandfather said nothing, walked purposefully into the house and came out shortly with his twelve-bore shotgun. He grabbed the dog by the collar and dragged him out of sight behind the barn. There was a single shot.

Then there was the time that I watched in awe as an elephant walked past the front gate of my grandparents' house. The elephant was part of a parade organised by a travelling circus as a publicity stunt.

My cousin Padraic was about my age, and during my visits we'd spend hours messing about in a nearby stream, building dams and catching pinkeens – tiny fish that we'd keep in a jam jar and eventually release back into the stream.

Before Christmas each year my parents and I would drive up to Cavan and stop off to visit various friends and relations along the way. Each stop involved being ushered into the 'good room' and served cups of tea, sandwiches and Christmas cake for the women and children and a glass of Paddy or Powers whiskey for my father and the man-of-the-house. In the 1960s it took almost three hours to drive the 120 km from Dublin to Cavan, the route taking us through towns and villages with Christmas trees decorated with large old-fashioned coloured bulbs. It was always dark as we drove back to Dublin, and I remember the excitement of lying across the back seat of the car, gazing out at the Christmas lights.

Losing my parents

Neither of my parents enjoyed good health. For most of his later life, my father suffered from angina and blocked arteries in his legs. He went for surgery in Cromwell Road Hospital in London in 1963, but the procedures that saved my life when I had a heart attack in 2011 had not yet been developed. My father died suddenly of a heart attack in July 1975. He was only fifty years old. He was a member of the team that pioneered cardiac care in Ireland and that made his passing even more poignant.

In my teenage years my mother suffered from what is now described as mental illness, but back then mental illness was not openly discussed with children. In hindsight I suspect that her illness may have been triggered by the menopause.

I remember visiting her in Saint Patrick's psychiatric hospital in Dublin, where she spent a couple of weeks undergoing electroconvulsive therapy. I don't think she ever fully recovered, and in later life she also suffered from what might have been irritable bowel syndrome. It was distressing to see such a strong, capable woman gradually become a shadow of her former self.

Her health gradually deteriorated to such an extent that her doctor recommended that she should no longer live alone and needed full-time care. I arranged for her to go to a nursing home in Clontarf, where she was well cared for until she sadly passed away in January 1996.

CHAPTER 2

Growing Up

Moving to Ireland

My father got a job as a pathologist with the newly established Irish National Blood Transfusion Service, and in 1951 we moved to Ireland.

I believe we lived for a time in Bray and later in a rented house on the west side of Howth near the tram line to Sutton Cross. In fact I was told that my pram once got stuck in the tram tracks and I was rescued just in time, but that seems like a tall tale.

My first permanent home was a three-bedroom bungalow at 14 Myrtle Grove in Merville Estate in Stillorgan, which, at the time, was an outer suburb on the southside of Dublin. I believe that we moved there in 1952 and at the time houses in Merville Estate were on sale for £1,950. My father's salary would have been approx. £300–350 per annum, i.e. the house cost six times his annual salary.

While there was no food rationing in 1950s Ireland, money was tight, and my parents lived frugally. My mother was a self-sufficient and resourceful woman – a great cook, seamstress, home decorator and gardener.

She was also a competent carpenter and built a wooden henhouse at the bottom of our suburban garden, in which she kept hens. She started with three 'layers': Sheila, Patricia and Annette named after the daughters of a relative in Cavan who had gifted the hens to my mother as day-old chicks.

One year my mother reared a few turkeys, but they were inclined to fly into neighbours' gardens, causing quite a stir. They survived until Christmas, but not beyond.

Primary school

My first school, Saint Brigid's National School in Cabinteely, was about 5 km from where we lived in Stillorgan. My teacher's name was Mrs Lally and I took the Number 63 bus home on my own from an early age. When I was about seven, my parents moved me to Saint Boniface's school, off Carysfort Avenue in Blackrock. I have no specific memory of the place except that the garden had box hedges, and to this day the distinctive smell of a box hedge evokes memories of my early childhood.

I spent my last couple of years of junior schooling at the Christian Brothers' Oatlands Primary School near Stillorgan village, within walking distance of home. I was never physically abused but corporal punishment was the norm, and I was regularly slapped with a heavy leather for the most minor misdemeanour. There was collection 'box' (it was actually a tin) on the teacher's desk, with a crude image of an African child and the message 'Give a penny for the black babies.' In fact, the donations were used to fund the thousands of Irish priests and nuns doing missionary work in Africa and Asia.

Sandymount High School
When I was about twelve, my parents enrolled me in Sandymount High School, which was on Herbert Road, a stone's throw from Lansdowne Road rugby ground (now the Aviva Stadium). Sandymount High School was radical for its time: it was non-denominational, coeducational, and privately owned by the Patrick Cannon, an educational reformer. The school next door, Marian College, was set up by the Marist Brothers at the invitation of the conservative Archbishop of Dublin, John Charles McQuaid, to effectively compete with Sandymount High School.

I have many happy memories of Sandymount High School, but academically I was a poor student. Because I didn't make the grade in Irish, I failed the Inter Cert (now the Junior Certificate) twice. However, I did go on to get an honours Leaving Certificate, which enabled me to study at Trinity College Dublin.

Sandymount High School was not a very sporty school, although the girls did play hockey and the boys played rugby. Unlike nearby Dublin schools such as Saint Michael's and Blackrock College, Sandymount High School didn't produce any Irish international players. In fact it was a struggle to find enough players to field a team.

Because the school was only a couple of hundred metres from the famous Lansdowne Road stadium, our Monday afternoon training sessions were on one of the two pitches at the back of the main stadium.

Our changing rooms were next to Lansdowne Rugby Club, which was then at one corner of the Havelock Square end. The changing rooms were also used by the Irish national team. Besides the showers, there were also enormous tiled communal baths.

My playing position was scrum half and, in those days, expediting the ball from the base of the scrum to the out half involved a diving pass. I can't remember the occasion, but I was about sixteen and a press photographer caught me in full flight.

Me getting the ball away with Charlie Bird emerging from the scrum.

One of my teammates that day was journalist Charlie Bird, who sat beside me in class for a couple of years. Charlie was already a fervent socialist, but like me, he was not a star student. After school he joined the national broadcaster, RTÉ, and eventually became chief news correspondent and, later, their Washington correspondent.

Trinity College Dublin

My father had ambitions for me to study marine biology at Trinity College Dublin, but my maths and overall science grades fell short of the entrance requirements. My only option was an arts course, then called general studies, which I began in October 1968. My three chosen subjects were English, economics and geography, and I was lucky to have three inspirational lecturers: poet Brendan Kennelly, economist Richie Ryan and my tutor, Dr Gordon Davies. With only six hours of lectures every week, students were expected to study on their own, but I was easily distracted, getting involved on the fringes of student politics as well as student clubs and societies.

My studies suffered, and in 1971 I opted not to repeat second year and I left college. I can't remember discussing my decision with my parents, but looking back I'm sure they must have been disappointed and concerned about my future career prospects.

While I did not graduate with a degree, my two years in Trinity had a positive influence on my life and exposed me to the political and social upheavals of the 1970s.

The Vietnam War was reaching a decisive stage, and anti-war movements were active in the US, UK and Ireland. In May 1968 France was engulfed by student street protests (which were violent even by French standards), and in Northern Ireland civil unrest spiralled out of control into fully-fledged sectarian warfare.

Like other universities, Trinity fostered political opinion of every sort, and the lunchtime debates on the steps of the dining hall always attracted a large crowd of hecklers and supporters. The two speakers were more often than not David Vipond, a passionate Maoist, and Joe Revington, a conservative Kerryman who went on to be a barrister and who was in his element on these occasions.

My pacifist tendencies made me supportive of organisations like the United Nations Student Association (UNSA) and the Irish Anti-Apartheid Movement. UNSA was ahead of its time in that it held a conference in 1970 on environmental protection at Saint Andrew's University in Scotland, which I attended at my own expense.

A South African, Kadar Asmal, was a Trinity law lecturer and exiled member of the African National Congress. He was also chairman of the Irish Anti-Apartheid Movement, whose meetings I attended in the Quaker Meeting House on Eustace Street. I supported the boycott of South African goods and protested the decision by the IRFU to tour South Africa. I resolved not to visit South Africa until Nelson Mandela was released, a promise to myself that I kept.

CHAPTER 3

Early Home Life

Our first TV set

Before December 1961 there was no national TV station in Ireland, so almost every house on our estate with a TV set had an aerial attached to a chimney on the roof. Aerials were pointed north to pick up BBC and UTV programmes being transmitted from Northern Ireland.

For whatever reason (probably cost) we didn't get a TV set until I was in my mid-teens, so on most Saturday nights we walked to our neighbours, the Flanagans, who had a TV. The three Dawsons and five Flanagans squeezed into their front room and watched *Rawhide, Bonanza, The Virginian, The Flintstones, The Lucy Show* and *The Beverly Hillbillies*. The black and white picture was often snowy, despite the best efforts of Mr Flanagan, who was constantly adjusting the rabbit-ears aerial that sat on top of the TV set.

When we eventually did get a TV set, my mother rented it from Irish TV Rentals in Dún Laoghaire.

Radio days

I have fond memories of being with my parents in the front room listening to a large Philips radio. I really looked forward to Friday evenings, when we'd tune into BBC long wave and listen to *The Archers* at 6.45 p.m. followed by *The Flying Doctor, The Navy Lark* and *Hancock's Half Hour*.

Theatre

Perhaps an early indicator of my creativity was staging puppet shows for the local kids in the hallway of our house in Stillorgan. I had no ambition to act – I was always much happier in a front-of-house or marketing role. During fifth year in school, I was the stage manager for a school play that was staged in the Saint Anthony's Theatre, on Merchants Quay in Dublin.

I often went to the theatre with my parents and looked forward to the annual visit to the Gaiety Theatre pantomime, which opened on Saint Stephen's Day. I was always envious of the people who sat in one of the private boxes, each with its own entrance door and individual chairs. Later in life I brought my family, including my mother, to a show in the Gaiety and I reserved a box – it was a special treat, although my daughter Elaine was very young at the time and she spent most of the show asleep on the carpet.

The Olympia was probably my favourite theatre; my father usually booked the cheapest seats in the gods, at the very top of the auditorium. Entrance to the gods was via a small lane that ran alongside the theatre. There were flights and flights of stairs to the top of the house, where we sat on wooden benches high above the stage. The John B. Keane play *The Field* debuted in the Olympia Theatre in 1965, with Ray McAnally as the Bull. I was lucky to see it during that run.

Backstage treat

Another memorable theatre experience was on my twelfth birthday. A colleague of my father was a niece of the well-known comedy actor Danny Cummins, and she arranged a backstage visit at the Theatre Royal after a show. The Theatre Royal opened in 1935 and seated 3,850, which made it the biggest theatre in Ireland and one of the largest in Europe. The theatre had its own dance troupe, The Royalettes, who

Theatre Royal. (National Library of Ireland)

were modelled on the famous Radio City Rockettes. Back then each performance included a movie and a musical revue featuring The Royalettes. The theatre was demolished in late 1962 and replaced by an ugly office block named Hawkins House, which in turn was demolished in 2022.

Cutting turf

During my early teens we teamed up with our neighbours the Flanagans to cut turf in the Wicklow Mountains, not far from the village of Glencree.

We rented a bank of turf bog for £50 from the landlord, Lord Powerscourt, with the aim of saving enough turf to keep both families in fuel for the coming winter. We started in early summer, with the men using a shovel-like tool called a slane to cut water-logged sods of turf, which we children laid out in long rows to dry. A few weeks after cutting we went back to the bog to turn the sods so the underside could dry. It was back-breaking work.

Turf 'footings'.

Every couple of hours we'd stop for mugs of tea brewed on a Bunsen burner. Tea never tasted as good as it did when we drank it there, sitting on the heather in the clean mountain air.

Assuming the weather was dry, we'd return to the bog in June or July to arrange the sods into footings, pyramid shaped bundles of turf about a metre high. Towards the end of summer (weather permitting) the footings would be consolidated into a large heap that would eventually be loaded onto a lorry, with half the load being delivered to each family. Our share would be carefully stacked up against the wall near our back door and covered with a tarpaulin to keep it dry. My mother lit a fire in the dining room most nights and in the 'good room' on weekends and special occasions.

Hill walking

Our family friend and neighbour Bonnie Flanagan was a keen hillwalker, and I'd often accompany her and her daughters on day-long walks, starting from her house on Oaktree Road in Stillorgan. We would walk past the Stillorgan Reservoir and the railway station up to the crossroads in Stepaside and then up the steep incline towards Three Rock Mountain. What was then the start of the countryside is now an expansive road network and motorway junction. In the words of W. B. Yeats everything is 'changed utterly: A terrible beauty is born', so much so that I now find it almost impossible to pick out any landmarks.

The top of Three Rock Mountain was pristine bog and granite outcrops overlooked by three very large rocks that gave the mountain its name.

Our route was tough going – there were a few narrow paths but much of the time we had to pick our way through heather and *fraochán* (a type of bilberry) bushes to avoid dark brown bog-water ponds. From Three Rock Mountain we walked across the Dublin Mountains and along a path that brought us down onto the Glencree Road. From there it was an easy downhill walk into the pretty village of Enniskerry, where we could take the Number 44 bus towards home.

DIY radio kit

In 1964 a commercial station named Radio Caroline started broadcasting pop music from a ship anchored in international waters off the Isle of Man. Radio Caroline was just one of several similar stations challenging the BBC's monopoly. I couldn't afford a radio, so I decided to buy a so-called crystal radio in kit form and build it myself.

My radio aerial was a 20 ft wire that ran from my bedroom window to a laburnum tree in the back garden. In addition to listening to commercial radio stations, I was able to eavesdrop on radio messages between ships and amateur home-radio operators known as ham operators.

Learning to Drive

My father got his first car, a Renault 4L, when I was about sixteen, and I taught myself to drive by reversing six feet down our driveway and then driving slowly forward for six feet – a manoeuvre I repeated and repeated over and over. When I turned seventeen, I got a provisional driving licence, which entitled me to drive with a qualified driver in the passenger seat. Later that year I passed my driving test and graduated to a full licence.

Moving to Howth

In anticipation of my father moving to work in the cardiac unit in the Mater Hospital on the northside of Dublin city, we moved to Howth in 1967. My parents bought a two-bedroom house at the top of the village, which my mother named Gable Cottage. She made a wooden hanging sign with Gable Cottage etched out of the wood with a hot poker. Many years after my mother's death, my daughter Amy made it her mission to acquire her Howth Granny's sign.

My parents' house in Howth: Gable Cottage, 43 Main Street.

Thanks to some detective work and persistence, she tracked down the current owner of Gable Cottage, who agreed to give Amy the original sign in return for a modern replica. Today the original hangs on my garden shed as a fitting reminder of my mother.

Holiday jobs

I had various holiday jobs over the years, including as a temporary driver, a shopping packer for H Williams Supermarket in Dundrum, a relief porter in Baggot Street Hospital, Santa Claus in Stillorgan Shopping Centre, a temporary Christmas postman and a relief cook on a trawler (more of that later).

Dublin Mountain hill walking.

CHAPTER 4

Hobbies and Influences

Sailing

In early 1962 a life-changing opportunity resulted from a casual chat between my father and a medical colleague, Dr Barbara Stokes, who was the paediatrician at Baggot Street Hospital, where my father was working at the time.

My father came home from work and announced that he'd had a conversation with Barbara Stokes and they both agreed it would be a good idea if I became crew on her son Andrew's small sailing dinghy. Andrew's father, Rory O'Hanlon, was a well-known gynaecologist and experienced yachtsman.

My first sailing experience was crewing on Andrew's 11 ft Heron class dinghy, which we sailed from the Royal Saint George Yacht Club in Dún Laoghaire Harbour, where his father was a member. Junior members had their own changing rooms 'below stairs', and the only time we were ever allowed into the clubhouse was during the annual regatta every summer.

That serendipitous meeting catapulted me into the world of Dublin's 'old money'. During the summer months Andrew and I hung out at the Dublin Bay Sailing Club junior section at the back of the west pier of Dún Laoghaire Harbour. Many of the fellow teens I met in the junior section became lifelong friends. Andrew and I sailed in weekly races in Dún Laoghaire, and his long-suffering mother drove us to various regattas, from Cobh to Bangor and everywhere in between. I became a competent enough sailor to be invited to crew on large yachts sailing out of Dún Laoghaire and Howth.

During my time in Trinity, I crewed for an experienced helmsman, Johnny Ross Murphy, on a team representing Ireland at the Firefly class university championships held in Nottingham. We didn't finish in the top three, but it was a memorable few days.

Once I started working and travelling, I was less able to commit to crewing on Tuesday and Thursday evenings and Saturday afternoons. As I spent more time abroad, I drifted (no pun intended) away from sailing. However, I still get a buzz stepping onto a boat.

The band

As well as Andrew, one of the other guys I met on the sailing circuit was Alan Winston, and we three became the founding members of a rock 'n' roll band called The Nuts. Alan was the lead guitarist, Andrew played rhythm guitar and I was drummer and sang a few songs. We practised in the mews of Andrew's family home in Clonskeagh.

My father gave me a loan of £50 for my first drum kit and I worked as a petrol pump attendant a couple of evenings a week at an Esso garage in Booterstown to repay him.

The Nuts expanded when two other sailing buddies, Hugh Cunniam and Garry Treacy joined as singer and bass player respectively. Because a couple of the lads were in boarding schools, the band only played during school holidays. Most of our gigs were private parties, yacht club or youth club hops. Our only claim to fame was playing as the support band at Stella House, one of the most popular Dublin dance venues in the sixties.

The band morphed into The Indication and eventually fizzled out when we all had college or career commitments. A few years ago, the original Nuts members got together with a couple of other musicians, and I played with them for a few years.

The band, 1969: Garry, Andrew, me, Hugh and Alan.

Ornithology

My father was a keen ornithologist, and he was a member of the Irish Ornithology Club (the predecessor of BirdWatch Ireland). He was friends with Fred Fox, who owned a large farm, Whitestown, near Tallaght, which ultimately became part of the suburban Dublin.

Both Fred and my father were keen wildfowlers, and during the winter months they would bring me on duck hunting trips along the Callows, flooded grassland along parts of the River Shannon. It was on these shooting trips that I learned fieldcraft and to respect the balance of nature. I also honed my bird recognition skills so that even after a half a century I can still identify a bird by its behaviour as well as its size and plumage.

My father was lucky enough to visit Lambay Island, off the east coast of Ireland, on a day trip organised by the Dublin Field Club. The private island is owned by the Baring family, currently headed by the 7th Baron Revelstoke. The ornithologists were invited to Lambay annually to conduct a bird count. It seems that the most surprising part of the trip was a glimpse of some wallabies, which were introduced to the island in the 1950s.

I went on a few bird watching trips with my father, including one to the Wexford Slobs Wildfowl Reserve on 24 March 1968 to see white-fronted geese and other migratory water birds. During our visit we commented on the number of helicopters and low-flying aircraft operating in the area around the Tuskar Rock Lighthouse. It was only later that we learned that the aircraft were searching for the wreckage of an Aer Lingus flight from Cork to London that had crashed into the sea off Tuskar with the loss of all sixty-one passengers and crew.

Heroes and villains

International politics is full of good intentions and double standards, and today's hero can become tomorrow's villain – Aung San Suu Kyi's fall from grace is a prime example.

The influencers and heroes who I'd like to meet at a dinner party include:
- Leonardo da Vinci
- Nelson Mandela
- David Attenborough
- Luciano Pavarotti

- Tom Crean
- Desmond Tutu
- John Hume
- Seamus Heaney
- Rosa Parks
- Michael Portillo

Archbishop Desmond Tutu

I was in Cape Town in June 2011 and was invited to attend a memorial service for Albertina Sisulu in Saint George's Cathedral. Affectionately know as Ma, Albertina Sisulu was the charismatic wife of Walter Sisulu, a senior ANC activist and peer of Nelson Mandela. She herself was an important political figure, committing herself to The Albertina Sisulu Foundation and working to improve the lives of children and older people.

Desmond Tutu, bishop, theologian and anti-apartheid and human rights activist.

One of my heroes, the former Archbishop of Cape Town Desmond Tutu, delivered the eulogy for Ma Sisulu.

After the service, the Archbishop was surrounded by reporters and photographers who fired questions in English, Afrikaans and Xhosa. When the interviews were ending, the Archbishop started to walk slowly down the aisle, at which point I made the decision that I would introduce myself and say hello. I explained that I was Irish and was an admirer of his. He said, 'I've visited Ireland many times and I'm a friend of your former president, Mrs Robinson. We're both members of The Elders, so we see each other regularly.'

We chatted for a few more minutes before he was ushered towards the door. What is most memorable about meeting Archbishop Tutu was the fact that he held my hand from the first handshake until we parted ways.

CHAPTER 5

Coming of Age

Married life

My personal life underwent major change when I met Jackie Ross at a party in a mutual friend's house. We started dating, and we got married on 18 September 1973. In today's terms we were young: I was twenty-three and Jackie was twenty. We were married in the Church of the Assumption in Howth, and we had our reception in the Saint Lawrence Hotel, opposite the harbour, which is now apartments. Jackie's sister Tonya was bridesmaid, and my friend Jim Leahy was my best man.

We stayed that night in Broc House Suites on Nutley Lane in Donnybrook, and the next day we flew to New York on an Aer Lingus charter flight organised by the student travel service, USIT. We had a couple of days in New York, staying in the Empire Hotel opposite the Lincoln Center on 63rd Street in Manhattan.

Wedding Day, 18 Sept 1973; Me, Jackie and Tonya.

We travelled by Greyhound bus on what now seems to be a very ambitious schedule, which included Montreal, Toronto, Niagara Falls (then the honeymoon capital of the world) and Lake George in Upstate New York.

On our return from the honeymoon, we lived in rented a house in Knocklyon, near Templeogue.

We returned to New York in the summer of 1974, I managed the USIT office and Jackie found work with another student organisation, the Council on International Educational Exchange. House prices in Ireland were starting to increase, and we had to pay £9,500 for our first house in Clontarf. However, we had managed to save £3,000 from our time in New York and this meant a relatively small twenty-year mortgage.

Children

Elaine was born in April 1975 and Amy arrived in June 1980. Amy was initially enthusiastically welcomed by her big sister. But after a few days the excitement waned, and Elaine said to Jackie, 'I love my little sister but when are you giving her back?'

I have been blessed to have three wonderful grandchildren, who live within a short distance of our house in Clontarf. Doris, born in February 2008 and Joseph, born in November 2014, are the children of Elaine and her husband, Felim. Mina, born in May 2008, is the daughter of Amy and her husband, Tommy.

My 'girls', Elaine, Jackie and Amy, November 2023.

All the grandchildren attended Saint Columba's National School, and Doris and Mina are now attending Mount Temple Comprehensive School, whose alumni include their own mothers and the members of some band named U2.

Jackie's family

My wife Jackie (née Ross) was born in Sligo in May 1953. Her father, Sydney Ross, was a New Zealander who served as an engineer in the British Merchant Navy during World War II. Her mother, Doris Osborne, was born in Dublin and she met Jackie's father in 1947, when he was on a ship based in Liverpool but had travelled to Dublin for so-called R&R leave. They were married in Dublin in February 1948 and moved to Sligo, where Jackie and her siblings, Alister and Tonya, were born. In 1959 her father transferred to a job in Dublin, and the family moved to a house in Clonskeagh on Dublin's southside.

All grown up

Jackie gave up work to be a full-time mother until the girls were older and more independent. At the time I was so concerned about my own career that I failed to recognise and appreciate the sacrifices that she made, both personally and financially. Mea culpa.

She went back to work as a temporary secretary for several years. One of her assignments was with the semi-state agency, Enterprise Ireland, charged with promoting Irish business overseas. In 1996 she successfully applied for a coveted permanent and pensionable role. By all accounts Enterprise Ireland was a very caring work environment and she really liked the people she worked with until she retired in 2017.

CHAPTER 6

Rugby in My Life

Ireland v England, 1963

On 11 March 1878, Lansdowne Road hosted its first international rugby fixture, against England, making it the world's oldest rugby union test venue.

My first introduction to international rugby was going to see Ireland play against England in 1963. The game ended nil all; high scoring games were rare then. The routine that day was a template for every other home international that I attended with my father. As soon as tickets went on sale, I would be dispatched to Fox's cigar shop on Lower Grafton Street, almost opposite the front gate of Trinity College, to buy the tickets. I never understood why a cigar and pipe shop sold rugby tickets, but it did.

I finished school at 12.30 p.m. on Saturdays and I'd hurry up Pembroke Road and meet my father in Mooney's pub on the corner of Haddington Road and Baggot Street. One of my father's colleagues, Maeve, and her husband Pat Timpson, joined us there and we'd all have a pint and a toasted ham and cheese sandwich before heading off to the match.

Maeve and Pat had seats on the small wooden stand at the Havelock Square end of the ground, but my father and I had only terrace tickets, so we got to the ground early to grab our favourite spot up against the wall near Havelock Square, with an uninterrupted view of the pitch. We were entertained by both the Army No. 1 band and the Garda Band, who would march around the pitch and stop every 150 metres or so and play for that section of the spectators. Those couple of hours would drag, waiting for kick-off, which was usually 3 p.m.

There was always good-humoured banter with visiting supporters and that also helped pass the time. The final part of pre-match entertainment was the last-minute arrival of the so-called sheepskin-coat-and-rug spectator brigade, who would take their place on wooden benches along the touch line, a couple of metres from the pitch. Their arrival always prompted a cacophony of wolf whistles and smart-ass comments from the crowd on the terraces. Finally, the teams ran out, the president arrived, the bands played the anthems, and the referee blew his whistle – the game was underway.

Supporters on the terraces were always more vocal than those sitting in the stands, so it was not uncommon to hear witty insults being hurled at underperforming or unpopular players.

Pre Ticketmaster ticket signed by Bob FitzGerald with whom I shared some wonderful Christmas dinners.

After one Irish winger managed to drop the ball on the try line, there was a yell of 'Jesus, Murphy, you couldn't score in a brothel!'

The post-match routine was also prescribed, starting with the walk up Haddington Road to Smyth's pub, where a full post-mortem would take place over multiple pints. If the game had been a Triple Crown or Five Nations decider and Ireland had been 'robbed' or trounced, you'd hear 'Sure maybe next year.'

Regardless of whether Ireland had won or lost, Pat Timpson would always have his own man of the match. His selection criteria were based on poor rather than superior performance – the merits of the players selection and play were analysed and argued over for hours and over a few more pints.

When I left school, I joined Old Wesley Rugby Club, whose ground was in Donnybrook. I played scrum half there for a couple of years and managed to make it to the 3As, but once I started working, I had to stop playing.

When I recently visited the marvellous International Rugby Experience in Limerick, I took part in several tests, including passing, kicking, line out and scrummaging. It was all good fun, and at the end of the visit a computer analysed my performance and calculated my best position. I was amazed that even after fifty years my position was computed to be … scrum half! Maybe I missed my calling?

Lions Tour of New Zealand, South Sea Hotel, Stewart Island.

Lions Tour of New Zealand

In 2005 I got some money from a pension investment and decided to go to New Zealand for some of the British and Irish Lions rugby tour. I booked tickets for a couple of mid-week games in Dunedin and Invercargill and the first test in Christchurch. While I was there, I stayed with friends and some of Jackie's New Zealand cousins.

I went to Dunedin, where I visited Jackie's Aunt Doreen and her husband, Tom, who lived close to where Jackie's father grew up. Tom was a retired university professor and a mad keen rugby fan who became very animated watching rugby on TV. He got so excited watching matches that for health reasons he was advised not to watch live games. The game had to be recorded and watched later after his wife had told him the final score.

After the game in Dunedin against Otago on 18 June, I drove down to Invercargill, a town at the very south of the South Island, where the Lions were due to play a local side, Southland. I had a couple of tickets for the game, but I had nowhere booked to stay, and the few hotels there were full. I got into conversation with the waitress in the Phat Cat Café, and a woman sitting at the next table said, 'You can have my son's room.' When I got to her house, a grumpy teenager was heading out the door to stay with a pal, having been unceremoniously kicked out of his room by a random Lions fan. Peace was restored when I gave him my spare ticket for the match.

I had a couple of days to kill before the game, so I booked a flight from

Invercargill to Stewart Island, 57 km off the South Island – next stop Antarctica. The twenty-minute flight was on a seven-seat aircraft, and when it landed, I took a taxi to the South Sea Hotel right next to the harbour. The reception desk was in the bar and when I walked in, the conversation stopped and then continued in hushed tones.

I was the only guest staying at the hotel, and after dinner I went back into the bar, where the locals were now much friendlier; I reckoned they had quizzed the barman as to who I was, where I was from and what I was doing there, so the next evening I was accepted as one of the lads.

Having worked on several small islands around the world, the common denominator is that the locals take a while to warm to strangers. Someone once cautioned me, 'Be careful, islanders tend to have big toes – they're easy to step on.' Good advice.

I had planned to go out with a guide on a night walk to try and see some Kiwis, which were still reasonably common on Stewart Island, but the weather was too wet. Kiwis and other land-nesting birds are under threat from possums that were introduced into New Zealand in the 1830s. One of the blokes at the bar explained that he was a professional possum hunter and earned a bounty for culling them.

The next morning, I went on a half-day sea-fishing trip before flying back to Invercargill for the game. The boat was about 25 ft, and the only other passengers were a honeymoon couple. We fished with heavy duty hand lines, and it wasn't long before I landed a large blue cod, quickly followed by about a dozen more. I was encouraged to take one of the fish back to the hotel, were the chef pan-fried it for my dinner that night.

The Lions played Southland in Invercargill on 21 June, winning 26–16, and the next day I flew up to Christchurch, where I met up with a pal of mine, Greg Macauley, who I'd invited to join me for the first test on 25 June. Greg lived in Sydney but happened to be in New Zealand to meet his wife, who was visiting family there.

The weather was awful: sleet, rain and a cold southerly gale – a miserable night. Our seats in the stadium were in the open, a few rows from the touchline, under the posts, so we got soaked. The game was testy from the kick-off, and within a few minutes Brian O'Driscoll was spear-tackled by two All Blacks and sustained a shoulder injury that ended his tour. I was sitting

Lions Tour to South Africa, Loftus Versfeld Stadium, Pretoria.

no more than 50 metres from the incident, and it was truly shocking to see such deliberate and dangerous foul play, which went unpunished.

Lions tour of South Africa, 2009

My work and sporting interests came together again in 2009, when I was working with Zambezi Airlines in Zambia and my trip coincided with the Lions tour of South Africa. I managed to get tickets for the second test match on 27 June in Pretoria.

I took an early-morning flight from Lusaka to Johannesburg, where it was a beautiful, cool, sunny winter's day. I hired a taxi from Johannesburg Airport to the famous Loftus Versfeld Stadium in Pretoria, where I met up with my hosts, three Afrikaans rugby fanatics. I followed them up a few flights of stairs to a members only bar dedicated to Springbok legends. I can only describe the place as very male and very white. I was asked what I'd like to drink and, given that it was only 11.30 a.m. and it was going to be a long day, I replied, 'I'll start with a small beer,' to which my host replied in disbelief, 'Ach, man, we've already had our beers. We're moving on to double rum and Coke.' He wouldn't take no for an answer, and I was inducted into the Rum and Coke Club.

The game was very tight. With only minutes to go, the score was 25–25, until Ronan O'Gara chased his own 'up and under' and gave away a penalty. Morne Steyn banged it through the posts from 53 metres to snatch a 28–25 victory.

Boys in Blue

I'm a member of Clontarf Rugby Club and a loyal Leinster season ticket holder. The Leinster home games are played at the RDS Arena in Ballsbridge, where I meet up with my auld pal Hugh Cunniam and a former colleague of his, Frank Murphy. Come hail, rain or shine we sit in the open South Stand and cheer on the Boys in Blue, many of whom are in the Irish international squad.

About five years ago I reluctantly stopped going to Ireland games in Lansdowne Road (now the Aviva Stadium) because of the ticket prices. Financial pressures mean that rugby clubs are forced to sell their ticket allocations for corporate entertainment, and this in turn has impacted on the atmosphere in the ground. The ultimate deciding factor was the constant interruptions of people coming and going to the bar (and then the loo) during games. So, while I must now watch the games on TV, I still have very fond memories of being in the old stadium and sharing precious time with my father.

Pubs closed, missing rugby during Covid.

CHAPTER 7

USIT Years

Airport representative

In 1971 a chance meeting with Jane McKeon, a friend of a friend, led to another life-changing opportunity. Jane worked for the Irish student travel organisation, USIT, and they needed an airport representative to oversee student charter-flight departures at Dublin and Shannon airports. I got the job, which mostly involved me being on hand at the check-in counters at Dublin and Shannon airports to reissue tickets and to hand over visa documents.

USIT Office, 11 St Stephen's Green.

Aer Lingus was the only handling agent. and another part of my job was to give them passenger lists for charter flights and then go to the boarding gate and collect a copy of the final manifest. USIT had no automated reservation system, which meant that I had to buy a scheduled flight ticket for the occasional overbooked passenger. Those were the days before low-cost air travel, and a one-way ticket on the student charter flight from Dublin to London cost £6.50, compared to £13.00 on Aer Lingus or BEA (which was absorbed into British Airways in 1974).

From mid-August till mid-October Irish students who spent the summer working in the US on the J-1 Visa programme began to return to Ireland. It was part of my role to meet and greet the charter-flight passengers arriving in Dublin from New York and Boston. The flights arrived very early in the morning, and I used to borrow my father's car and drive from my home in Howth to Dublin Airport on the back roads via Baldoyle and Cloghran.

In the 1950s the terminal was used for both arrivals and departures; the so-called North Terminal was added in 1959 for arriving passengers. Thankfully the original terminal and its roadway approaches have been preserved – take a look if you are walking to the D Pier gates in Dublin Airport. It's not just the physical buildings that are different; air travel was expensive, and aircraft were generally smaller than they are today. Fewer passengers meant less crowded terminals and a much more pleasant travel experience. Back then there were no security checks at airports; after check-in you walked to the gate and boarded your flight.

Dublin Airport was the home of the Collar of Gold restaurant located on the first floor of the terminal building, overlooking the tarmac. In the 1950s and sixties, the Collar of Gold was a hugely popular venue for dinner dances and private parties.

The 'new' terminal (now T1) opened in 1972, and USIT was the first non-airline to have a ticket desk at the airport to provide information and sell tickets to student passengers.

Shannon Airport

J-1 student work visas were issued by the US Embassy in Dublin, but there were often backlogs, meaning that sometimes students only received their visa a day or two before travel. Dublin-based students could collect their visa from the US Embassy, but this wasn't always possible for students living in the south and west of the country who wanted to board at Shannon.

It was part of my job to deliver J1 visas and passports to students at Shannon Airport – Shannon was a mandatory stopover for transatlantic flights until 2008. The routine was to oversee the check-in at Dublin Airport, hop on the charter flight as far as Shannon and literally run along the long corridor that linked Arrivals and the check-in desks. When I got to the check-in, I'd be met by anxious students waiting for their passports. I'd quickly hand over their passports and visas, so they could check in and board the flight to New York or Boston.

Once the flight had departed from Shannon, my next challenge was to get back to Dublin so I could do the whole thing over again the next day (and almost every day in the month of June). My strategy was to go to the car hire counters in Arrivals and ask each of them, 'Do you need a car returned to Dublin?' The deal was that I'd drive the car back to their depot at Dublin Airport and they would pay for the petrol. It worked every time. If I was ready to leave Shannon before 5 p.m. I'd usually stop at Durty Nelly's Pub in

Bunratty for one of their famous toasted cheese, onion and ham sandwiches. Attitudes to drink driving were very different back then so I'd usually have a pint before driving back to Dublin, which back then took about four hours.

Gordon Colleary

After an interview with the USIT general manager, Adrian Foley and the MD Gordon Colleary, I joined USIT on a permanent basis in October 1971 as counter sales manager, based at the head office in 11 Saint Stephen's Green. I had no professional qualifications or managerial experience, yet I was given the job of managing six staff (all women) in a busy sales office. There was no recruitment process and no formal training – I was just expected to get on with it.

Gordon Colleary.

All of this must be viewed in historical context. USIT was founded by a recently graduated UCD student named Gordon Colleary, who these days would be considered a maverick entrepreneur. Gordon was involved in the Union of Students in Ireland. under whose auspices he set up a 'travel bureau' that evolved into USIT. In the late sixties and early seventies, the principal activity was the US J-1 work visa programme, which involved sending over 10,000 Irish students on charter flights to the US, where they worked for the summer to earn their college fees.

Under Gordon's leadership, USIT expanded into mainstream travel with its travel agency named Usitravel, an incoming tour operation called Usitours, and sun-holiday tour operator called Blueskies. This expansion required more office space, and at one stage there were USIT related businesses or offices in 4, 5, 7 and 11 Saint Stephens Green.

Gordon empowered people. His mantra was typically 'Great idea! You do it, I'll find the money.' While there was sometimes a clash of styles, we made a good team, and together we were the nucleus of USIT's expansion into the UK market and beyond. Gordon encouraged my self-taught flair for using technology to automate business processes, and while I was not a programmer or developer, I was able to identify situations where repetitive tasks could be automated. My first venture was to design a programme that allowed USIT to automate its travel insurance sales returns to the insurance broker. In the early

1980s Gordon supported me when I designed a programme to issue European rail tickets and a charter-flight reservation system.

Gordon and his wife, Mairin, were also supportive to me on a personal and family level. An example of this was when I was marooned in Zürich and Gordon braved a snowstorm to visit my daughter Elaine in Temple Street Children's Hospital when she recovering from an appendix operation.

Growth of student travel

In the 1960s an international coalition of like-minded student organisations in Europe began to operate a network of inter-European student charter flights under an umbrella organisation named the Student Air Travel Association. Before the development of low-cost air travel in the mid-1980s, cheap fares involved having to buy a return ticket with strict minimum and maximum stay regulations.

The concept of student charter flights evolved because students were looking for one-way fares that would allow them flexibility around length of stay and mode of travel. Many would choose a one-way flight and take the train or bus in the other direction.

The international student travel community had a semi-automated reservation system based in Copenhagen and a common ticket that allowed each student travel operator to sell seats on another operator's flight.

Many student travel companies collapsed because they failed to adapt to changes in the market, and USIT moved to fill the void by expanding into the UK, Europe and New Zealand. The only major market left was the United States, and in 2001 USIT moved to acquire an established organisation, Council Travel. Unfortunately, the timing could not have been worse; USIT completed the purchase in early September 2001, just days before the World Trade Center attacks shocked the world and Americans became very reluctant to travel overseas. USIT managed to continue trading into the New Year, but in January 2002 it finally went bankrupt.

Some individual coun-try operations were acquired by local management and reinvented themselves; some are still trading.

International Student Travel Conference

The International Student Travel Conference (ISTC) was an international body whose worldwide membership consisted of not-for-profit national student travel companies. The ISTC established a full-time secretariat based in Zürich, managed by Ursi Silberschmidt.

Gordon supported my candidacy as the part-time ISTC project manager to promote the development of the International Student Identity Card (ISIC) worldwide. The ISTC funded the production of a pocket-sized Discount & Benefit Guide for ISIC card holders. It was a very ambitious project that involved asking and cajoling member organisations to send details of ISIC discounts in their respective countries. Members were given the option of having a bespoke cover with their own language and branding. The final print run was over a million, with forty different covers, which were then shipped all over the world – phew! The guide was well received but, thankfully, future editions were managed by the secretariat.

Part of my role as project manager was to assist member organisations to promote the ISIC and negotiate student discounts. These assignments took me to Canada, Australia, New Zealand, Costa Rica, Nicaragua, Brazil and Iran.

I was lucky enough to be part of the USIT delegation at the annual confer-ences that took place in Portugal, Hungary, Australia, the US, Venezuela and the Philippines. My final conference was in Krakow in Poland in February 1990, where we celebrated the release of Nelson Man-dela with the South African delegation.

Student Travel Guide.

CHAPTER 8

Ryanair

Taking flight

It started with a phone call from my pal Greg Jones, asking if I was interested in being 'spoken to' about joining a new airline Tony Ryan was setting up. Greg knew Tony from his days working for Guinness Peat Aviation (GPA). I felt it was the time to move on from USIT, so I took the first step and went for a clandestine meeting with Tony Ryan at his home, Kilboy Estate in County Tipperary. There were a couple of other people there, including Tony's son Declan and Derek O'Brien. Derek and I recognised each other from the time he had been an Aer Lingus duty manager at JFK while I was working for USIT. We were briefed on the plan to launch Ireland's first low-cost airline, which would compete with the national carrier, Aer Lingus.

The meeting went well, and within a couple of days I was invited to meet the Ryanair chairman, Arthur Walls, to talk about the position of sales and marketing manager of the new airline. The meeting took place in Arthur's office on the second floor of the iconic Clerys department store on O'Connell Street in Dublin, where he was chief executive at the time. By the end of the meeting, I was offered the job and became the fifth employee of the nascent airline.

Things moved very quickly after that, and in early February 1986 I made the decision to resign from USIT. Gordon Colleary was very magnanimous and helpful and agreed that I could start with Ryanair the following week. The airline's first 'office' was on the garden level of 32 Wellington Road in Ballsbridge, home of the recently appointed Ryanair chief executive, Eugene O'Neill.

There I met the other members of the start-up team, including Declan McAdams, who became the charter manager, and other key staff. We worked around a large kitchen table while Eugene's wife, Abigail, looked after her young children and graciously brewed endless cups of coffee. It's hard to believe that the first route-planning exercise involved using Eugene's kids tatty school atlas and a ruler.

Within a couple of weeks, we'd moved into short-term serviced offices in Clifton House on Fitzwilliam Street, and the management team had grown to include operational functions such as flight operations, ground operations, engineering and cabin services.

Recruitment

The next task was to recruit multifunctional customer service agents (CSAs). The concept of multitasking had been successfully used by America West airlines, where CSAs were trained to work as cabin crew, call centre agents, ticket sales agent and at check-in, depending on where they were needed.

In 1986 the unemployment rate in Ireland was 16 per cent, which explained the extraordinary response to our recruitment advertising – the post office van was literally delivering sacks of mail. By the time applications closed, we had more than 9,500 applicants for twelve jobs.

We couldn't possibly have opened and read every application, so 250 envelopes were randomly selected, reviewed, and eventually whittled down to 125 interview candidates. The interviews took place over the Easter holiday weekend and the roles were allocated the following week.

We made it happen

In early April 1986, the new offices at 3 Dawson Street were ready, and one of my roles was to set up a reservation system and open a ticket office so we could start taking bookings and issuing tickets. The launch date was less than six weeks away by then.

At that time, Ryanair was already operating the Waterford to Gatwick route using a nineteen-seat aircraft and a manual booking system. The expansion of the business required an automated system that could provide real-time seat availability. As a stop-gap measure USIT agreed to loan us six desktop computers loaded with their charter-flight reservation system software that I had developed; two terminals were allocated to the ticket office counter and the remaining four were located in the 'call centre'. The Ryanair office in London wasn't automated, so they set up a card index system to manage a small block of seats on every flight. Every night, passenger names were faxed to the Dublin office and inputted into the USIT system. The server memory was only 10 MB, a tiny fraction of the memory of a modern mobile phone, and demand was such that we were fast reaching capacity.

I negotiated an agreement with British Airways to use their BABS reservation system, and a couple of weeks later we printed off all the bookings on a Friday evening and hopped on the last flight to Heathrow. A small team of us worked all day Saturday and Sunday in a British Airways office inputting the bookings to BABS so that on Monday morning the offices in Dublin, London and Waterford were all live.

We now had a reservation system but no dedicated phone number, so I was tasked with getting a memorable 'vanity' phone number for the call centre. I went to the Telecom Éireann office on Dame Street and explained that I had just started a new job and I needed a memorable number like 88 88 88, only to be told that such numbers were reserved for taxi companies. I pleaded and pleaded and eventually succeeded in getting 77 44 22 – one small step forward. Just a few months later, Telecom Éireann added a 6 to all Dublin city centre numbers and that was the end of my 'sexy' number.

The weeks before the inaugural flight were hectic. We had to appoint an advertising agency, erect airport signage, rent office space, negotiate contracts with travel agents, arrange media interviews, design the CSA uniforms, print timetables, posters, manuals and tickets (no e-tickets back then), deliver pilot

We were still operating this 19-seater Bandeirante aircraft when I joined in 1986.

Ryanair sponsored a visit of this Sunderland to the Foynes Flying Boat Museum; branding was done at the Chatham Naval Dockyard on the Thames.

and cabin crew training and licensing, and installing new interiors to our two HS 748 aircraft. Many staff recruits were in their twenties, with no airline experience, but nevertheless it all started to come together just in time for the planned inaugural date, 23 May 1986.

Media launch

The official press launch was held in the Westbury Hotel in early May. At the time, the duopoly carriers, Aer Lingus and British Airways, both charged £209 for a standard unrestricted return fare between Dublin and London, while Ryanair planned on charging £99 return. About an hour before the press launch, we got word that Aer Lingus had introduced a return fare for £95. Not to be outdone, the press release and the slide show presentation were hastily changed, and Ryanair announced a return fare of £94.99, one penny less than Aer Lingus. Revenue management had yet to evolve, and so the communications strategy was '£94.99 return, every seat, on every flight on every day.' In modern airline yield-management practice this type of pricing strategy would be financial madness, but then it was a necessary evil to get the airline noticed.

As Ireland evolved into an open economy, the old state companies such as Aer Lingus were increasingly being perceived as staid and anti-competitive. On the other hand, Ryanair was seen as young (the CEO, Eugene O'Neill, was just thirty-two), cheeky and progressive – a private business taking on the state monolith.

At first Aer Lingus didn't take us very seriously, but a few weeks after our launch, the Department of Transport – which we jokingly referred to as the Aer Lingus Downtown Office – contacted us. They claimed to have received complaints about us fraudulently advertising our Dublin–Luton flights as flights to London. We put a stop to this nonsense by pointing out that Luton Airport was designated by IATA as a London area airport.

A couple of days before the inaugural flight, all the staff (by this stage we were up to about sixty) gathered for a party in a Dublin nightclub, Howl at the Moon. The scale of what we were about to embark on hit home when one of the speakers said, 'This is a very special party, because once we start flying, we'll never all be in the one place at the one time ever again.'

Inaugural flight

Sunrise was at 5.14 a.m. on Friday 23 May 1986 but I was awake before then and in Dublin Airport before 6 a.m. to get the check-in desk open for the inaugural flight to London Luton – FR200, departing at 7.20 a.m.

Because Aer Lingus was the sole handling agent at Dublin Airport, there was a battle to persuade Aer Rianta (the airport manager) to allow us to self-handle, i.e. check in and board passengers as well as carry out ramp activities such as baggage loading, fuelling, marshalling and dispatch.

Because all the check-in desks with conveyor belts were leased to Aer Lingus, we had to improvise and use a tour operator desk at the far end of what is now Terminal 1.

An old-fashioned baggage weighing scale was placed beside the desk and tagged bags were then manually loaded onto a trolley and brought down to the ramp in a public lift.

The first flight was fully booked with forty-four passengers, of which twenty were inaugural guests and the remainder where the first revenue passengers. A small queue had already formed by the time check-in opened, and the first passenger moved forward to check in.

'I made a booking, but I need to pay for my ticket.'

We quickly found his name on the manifest and asked him for £59 for the one-way ticket.

'I only have sterling cash,' he said.

We'd no cash float, so I handed over the change from my wallet.

Despite all our preparations we'd not counted on the very first passenger paying in sterling and having to give the change in punts – a real live example of Murphy's Law.

It was rather chaotic, but after about forty minutes the check-in was completed, and the passengers were making their way to the boarding gate in the Pavilion boarding area. Watching the procedure was my old boss from USIT, Gordon Colleary, who afterwards presented me with a bottle of champagne and said, 'Congratulations, but today is the start of the end of our business.' Those were very prophetic words, because the advent of low-cost carriers, the growth of the internet and development of online payment systems resulted in a dramatic change in the distribution model.

I went down to the boarding gate to oversee the boarding and watched with a mixture of relief and pride as the steps were removed, engines started up and the aircraft started to taxi out. It was then that things started to unravel.

'Who's that man wandering around the ramp?' I asked the gate agent.

It turned out to be one of the VIPs who'd gone to the loo and missed the boarding call. We quickly contacted operations, and a few minutes later the aircraft was taxiing back to the stand. The steps were repositioned, and the VIP was put safely on board.

Commemorative Galway Crystal.

The rest of that day was uneventful. The aircraft operated a so-called W pattern – Dublin–Luton–Waterford–Luton–Dublin – and arrived back in Dublin at 9 p.m. that evening.

I eventually got home and into bed just after midnight – exhausted but elated. I looked at the clock and only then did I grasp the fact that in less than six hours the operation would start all over again, and again, and again. Over thirty-five years later, the first Ryanair departure to London is at 6.05 a.m. and there are direct flights from Dublin to 113 destinations in the UK, Europe and North Africa.

Flying fowl

The 1987 the Ireland v France rugby international was played in Lansdowne Road on 21 March, coinciding with the Saint Patrick's Day weekend. A French tour operator chartered one of our BAC1-11 jets to fly French rugby supporters from Toulouse to Dublin and back; the so-called 'ferry legs' in the opposite direction were used by a group of ladies on a diocesan pilgrimage to Lourdes.

The tour operator insisted that we offer a meal service on the flights, but because Ryanair didn't offer meals on scheduled flights the airline had no catering department, so I was delegated to find a solution. This involved ordering disposable meal boxes and sourcing a catering company to provide the food.

At the time the only flight kitchen at Dublin Airport was owned by our competitor, Aer Lingus, so that wasn't an option. I was introduced to Campbell Catering and contracted with them to provide cold meals on the flights to and from Toulouse. The Campbell Catering facility wasn't equipped to prepare the 240 meals needed, so for some reason (which I've forgotten) the meals were prepared in the kitchen of the Freemasons' Hall in 17 Molesworth Street.

Because this was my project, I travelled on the flight as a supernumerary crew member to observe the in-flight service and assist the cabin crew with the catering.

The two-hour flight from Dublin to Toulouse was largely uneventful; the ladies seemed to enjoy their meal, and the flight was smooth. However, at one point one of the passengers asked a crew member if the pilot could give some information about the route. Because the cockpit crew were Romanians with heavy accents, they didn't normally make passenger announcements (PAs); the protocol was that one of the cabin crew would make the PA.

I went into the cockpit and said, 'Captain, some of the passengers are asking where we're flying over'. The captain leaned forward, looked out the windscreen and replied, 'France.'

The flight back from Toulouse to Dublin was much less mundane and a lot noisier. The rugby supporters were mostly men who had clearly been in the airport bar before the flight. They were dressed in French rugby jerseys, rugby regalia and ubiquitous French berets. After take-off the cabin crew served the meals, but they were largely untouched – the passengers had brought their own baguettes, hunks of cheese and assorted pâtés and cured meats. They didn't seem impressed with our menu or inclined to eat food from a plastic box!

It was only after landing at Dublin Airport that the cabin crew noticed that a live cockerel had been smuggled on board in a wicker basket. Back then it was not uncommon for visiting French fans to bring a live cockerel into Lansdowne Road and release him onto the pitch before the game. I always wondered if there was more coq au vin on restaurant menus the following week!

Moving on

Tony Ryan's vision of a low-cost, high-quality airline proved to be an unsustainable business model, and the airline operated at a loss during the start-up phase. Michael O'Leary joined Ryanair in 1988 with a mandate to fix the problem.

By 1989 the start-up phase was over, and I was becoming disenchanted by many of the changes Michael was making, especially relating to customer service. In mid-July I resigned to move on to the next phase of my career.

I am lucky to have been involved in Ryanair at a time of such dynamic change both in aviation and the Irish economy, and I'm proud when I see Ryanair aircraft at airports throughout Europe. I believe that Ryanair's challenge to the status quo and its can-do attitude played a significant part in regenerating the Irish economy.

My farewell gift.

CHAPTER 9

Becoming a Consultant

Counterpoint

As soon as I had made the decision to leave Ryanair, I set up Counterpoint Ltd, which I used as an umbrella for my yet to be defined consultancy business.

Gordon Colleary came to my rescue by asking me to work on some USIT projects that had been on the long finger. Looking back, I think that they were probably 'makey-uppy' assignments to help me out – another example of his generosity of spirit.

I needed to get other business, so I followed up on a lead I'd been given by Philip Heneghan, one of the directors of CHL Consulting. Philip suggested I meet with Winair, a small regional airline based in Saint Martin, in the Caribbean.

On 7 November 1989 I flew from London to Antigua and the next day I went on to Saint Martin, where I met with the CEO of Winair. I was disappointed to learn that he didn't have a role for me, but he kindly gave me a free return ticket to fly to the nearby island of Saba. The airport in Saba is perched on the edge of an extinct volcano and is the shortest commercial

Saba – the worlds shortest commercial runway – it's more like an aircraft carrier!

runway in the world. Landing involves flying towards the cliffs and making a sharp last-minute turn to land. I spent a couple of hours on Saba before flying back to Saint Martin.

From Saint Martin I flew on LIAT Airlines to Trinidad, where I met with some Indian students who had studied in Dublin and were looking for USIT's help to set up a student travel business in Trinidad. Nothing came of the plans, but I was grateful to have had the opportunity to see something of the Caribbean.

For a few months I based myself in the CHL offices in Dublin and worked in a 'back-stop' role on several reports that Philip was producing for tourist boards.

Counterpoint morphed into Dacon Ltd (Dawson Associates), which I founded in March 1992 and which I continued to use to conduct by consultancy projects for the following thirty-plus years.

Air Support Ltd

In early May 1992 I set up a separate company, Air Support Ltd, to act as an airline general sales agency (GSA) and travel wholesaler. The impetus for this move was an approach from French airline Air Littoral, who wanted a GSA to promote their planned flights from Dublin to Paris and Nice.

I needed a city centre office in a nice part of town and was lucky to move into first-floor offices on the corner of Duke Street and Grafton Street that had recently been vacated by Delta Air Lines; the address was 21 Grafton Street, but the entrance was a doorway on Duke Street.

It seems bonkers now, but I used to drive from home into the centre of Dublin and park in a basement car park on Drury Street, a short walk to the office.

My office on the first floor had a window that opened onto the hustle and bustle of Grafton Street. In the summer there was a cacophony of sound from numerous buskers and street artists, including Thom McGinty, AKA the Diceman. While most of the musicians were talented, there was one busker who played a large saw that sounded like a wounded animal.

I employed a secretary and a couple of French-speaking staff and used the office as a base for my consultancy business. The Dublin–Paris route was very competitive, and Air Littoral struggled with very low load factors. On the other hand, the weekly Saturday flight from Dublin to Nice was supported by tour operators and did much better.

Air Littoral decided to pull out of the Irish market, and our office overheads were no longer sustainable. Thankfully, USIT needed office space, and they took over the lease (and most of my staff) and I worked from home and from offices in Pembroke Street, which I shared for a time with Derek O'Brien after he left Ryanair.

Postscript: In 1997 I set up a new company, Air Support Ireland Ltd, in partnership with Bob Evans of Dún Laoghaire Travel, based at his office in Pembroke Road. The company acted as a consolidator (i.e. a wholesaler) for KLM and Air France, issuing discounted long-haul tickets to travel agents. Sadly this arrangement ended in tears after a couple of years and Bob took on my share of the business.

CHAPTER 10

Treasured Traditions

Festive season
With few exceptions I've always woken on Christmas morning at home in Dublin and I enjoy the run-up to Christmas as much as the day itself. The search for the perfect Christmas tree signalled the beginning of the festive season. That was followed by office parties (that usually clashed with school nativity plays), furtive present shopping and the marathon pre-Christmas trip to the supermarket.

Childhood Christmas
During my own Santa years, the weeks before Christmas were filled with anticipation and ritual. The Saturday before Christmas meant a visit to see Father Christmas in Tierney's in Dún Laoghaire. My father worked on Saturday mornings, so my mother and I took the 46A bus to Dún Laoghaire to meet my father after work. The Father Christmas in Tierney's was the real Santa Claus and not some imposter in an ill-fitting suit.

Our Christmas tree was set up in our living room and was festooned with lantern shades depicting Disney cartoon characters. The lighting set went missing when we moved house and I've never been able to find a replacement.

On Christmas morning my mother lit the fire before we went to Mass, and when we got home neighbours would drop in for a drink (typically a sherry) before Christmas dinner.

At some stage we started to visit some friends of my parents in Clonskeagh, Terrance and Aileen Chapman and their children, Suzanne and Charles. The Chapmans were generous hosts – there was a seemingly bottomless saucepan of mulled wine and endless trays of cocktail sausages. By early afternoon the party would wind up and we'd drive home; these were the days when it was still common practice to get behind the wheel after a couple of drinks.

It happened that the Chapman children were friendly with Jackie and her sister, Tonya, and when we got married, we kept up the tradition of visiting the Chapmans until we established our own Christmas traditions.

When our girls were young, we would go into town on Christmas Eve to look at Switzers' window displays that depicted classic Christmas scenes and to see the live-animal crib outside the Mansion House on Dawson Street.

Christmas Eve

The perfect Christmas Eve was a cold, sunny morning, a promenade up and down Grafton Street (you'd never know who you'd meet), followed by an Irish coffee in the snug space downstairs in Neary's (still my favourite pub in Dublin) and the walk back to Pearse Street Station to get the DART home. En route to the DART we'd stop and have a chat with, and donate to, the Black Santa outside Saint Ann's Church on Dawson Street. By the time we arrived home, the challenge was to get the girls into bed and asleep before Santa visited.

As time went on and our extended family grew, and the routines changed, Jackie and I would visit our friend Stephen Feldman in Rathmines to wish him a happy birthday, and then we'd meet the rest of the family for Christmas Eve lunch, often in Milano, where they serve gluten-free pizzas. In later years Amy and Elaine started their own traditions on Christmas Eve, but we would often meet up to exchange presents.

On a few occasions we were lucky to get tickets for the annual Service of Nine Lessons and Carols at Saint Patrick's Cathedral, where the service begins with a boy chorister singing 'Once In Royal David's City', his voice filling the beautiful space.

Christmas in Chadwick's

I can't remember how it started but Christmas lunch hosted by our friends the Chadwick's has been a Dawson family tradition for over twenty years.

Brian and Deidre Chadwick were neighbours when we lived in our first home in Chelsea Gardens in Clontarf, before they moved to a Georgian house on the North Circular Road near one of the entrances to the Phoenix Park. It's the perfect Christmas house – log fire, massive Christmas tree and a large mahogany dining table that comfortably sits fifteen people.

What started with Jackie, me and our two very young daughters being invited for lunch morphed over the years to invitations to the extended Dawson family.

The duties were shared, the Dawson's being responsible for providing and cooking a 9+ kg turkey, complemented with cranberry sauce and stuffing balls, while the Chadwicks looked after the rest. Deirdre's mother, Maud (sadly no longer with us) provided a wonderful Christmas pudding. The cooked turkey was transported from Clontarf to Chadwick's in the boot of the car, wrapped in tinfoil, a duvet and pillows, so by the time it came time for carving it was well and truly rested (in every sense of the word).

After a welcome glass of champagne, we'd move to the dining room. I'd don an apron and start carving the turkey and ham, ably assisted by Brian and Deirdre's daughter, Lucy. The service is executed with military precision.

Deirdre's late father, Bob FitzGerald, was in all senses of the word, a true gentleman. In respect for his seniority, Bob was asked to say grace. There were calls for *ciúnas*, and when everyone stopped chattering, Bob would stand and say grace, often in Latin.

Christmas Eve 2018. Felim, Joseph, Elaine, myself, Doris, Jackie, Tommy, Mina and Amy.

PART II

CHAPTER 11

Bitten by the Travel Bug

'The Minister for External Affairs of Ireland requests all whom it may concern to allow the bearer, a citizen of Ireland, to pass freely and without hindrance and to afford the bearer all necessary assistance and protection.'

I was eighteen when I first read and reread the words inside the front cover of my first passport. They conjured up imaginary trips to far-flung corners of the world, where having such a passport would offer the type of protection reminiscent of a different era. Thankfully I have never had to rely on diplomatic protection, although I must admit that on more than one occasion my 'neutral' Irish passport has been very useful. Being a former colony rather than a former colonialist is also a great help.

The European Union passports are not so exotic – at most borders, travellers with the ubiquitous burgundy passport get no more than a nod, and the practice of stamping passports has all but disappeared, in Europe at least.

I didn't know it then, but my interest and curiosity about the world began at a very early stage. My father was responsible for instilling in me the need to see for myself and not to accept everything I was told at face value. He inculcated in me a tolerance of other peoples and cultures, which I have tried to retain throughout my life.

During my childhood we made regular visits to my maternal grandparents' home in Drumalee, just outside Cavan town. We didn't have our own car until the early 1960s, so my father used to borrow or hire a car.

On one occasion we hired a Henkel bubble car, a curious three-wheeled vehicle with a single Perspex door which opened outwards. The driver and one passenger sat in front, and I sat on the tiny single seat in the back. We hired it from a company in Lad Lane and I remember thinking it was so sophisticated, whereas today it probably wouldn't be allowed on the road. On one trip to Cavan we did some touring around the area and visited Swanlinbar to see the source of the River Shannon. What a disappointment! In the years to come I would see the Shannon further downstream and could not reconcile this magnificent river with that trickle of water in a boggy field.

Boat and coach to London

When I was about ten years old, my mother took me to London to visit my Aunt Patsy, who lived in Hounslow, in West London, near Heathrow Airport. We travelled overnight on the British and Irish Steam Packet Company boat (later B&I and subsequently Irish Ferries) from Dublin's North Wall docks to Liverpool. We had a cabin for the overnight crossing, and I remember waking the next morning to see the ship being manoeuvred through the locks into its berth on the River Mersey.

We then travelled on to London by National Express coach, with a lunch stop in Stratford-On-Avon – no motorway service stations in those days. We were exhausted by the time we finally got to Victoria Coach Station in London, but the excitement of the journey and being in London made it all worthwhile.

My mother and aunt took me to see various tourist attractions such as Madame Tussauds and the London Planetarium, but the most memorable was going to Trafalgar Square to feed the pigeons.

Parents take their children on trips to both relive and share part of their own childhood, but it's amazing how little of these experiences their kids remember. I reminded my daughter Elaine of trips to Disneyland, New York and Canada when she was under ten, but only a few years later, the memories had faded.

My Uncle Willie Usher was an avionics engineer with British European Airways and I loved to talk to him about aeroplanes. When I stayed at their house in Hounslow, I used to spend hours looking out their back bedroom window to watch the aeroplanes flying low on approach to London Airport; Irish people of a certain age always referred to Heathrow as London Airport.

Over the years the aeroplanes changed – after the big turbo props came the Trident, Comet, and Boeing 707, followed by the Boeing 747 and twin-engine Boeings and Airbuses. The liveries changed over the years as airlines merged, changed name or simply updated their corporate identity.

CHAPTER 12

All at Sea 1967

My father had a friend who had a friend who worked for Bord Iascaigh Mhara, the sea fisheries development body in Ireland. It seemed that they were looking for a replacement cook on a research vessel named *Cú Na Mara*, which was based in Kinsale, County Cork. At the time I could just about make an omelette and knew the basics of cooking, but that didn't qualify or prepare me for the job of feeding seven men on a forty-foot fishing boat. Despite this, I got the job and in early June I took the train and bus from Dublin to Kinsale. This was the Summer of Love in California and the Scott McKenzie song 'San Francisco' was playing on every radio station; I even had one of those flower power shirts.

Having been introduced to the crew, I was given the food kitty and told to go to the supermarket to buy provisions for the following few days.

Coming from a small family where my mother did all the food shopping, I wasn't used to shopping for eight crewmembers, especially bearing in mind that we were going to be at sea, where it wasn't possible to pop out for an extra pint of milk.

The *Cú Na Mara* was tied up to a pier close to the newly built Trident Hotel in Kinsale, and from there we travelled out beyond the Old Head of Kinsale, doing research on various types of lobster pots.

The morning after I arrived, I was woken up at 5 a.m. by the movement of the *Cú Na Mara* leaving port and heading out to sea. My first job was to prepare tea and toast for the men. No sooner had I washed up than they were looking for a cooked breakfast.

Except for a university student doing marine biology, the rest of the crew were tough trawlermen who liked plain food and plenty of it. Breakfast was typically a couple of fried eggs, rashers, sausages and black pudding, all washed down by endless mugs of tea. We got through a large sliced pan at every meal.

The crew weren't very adventurous eaters; most meals consisted of meat, meat and more meat, but given that our mission was to test lobster pots, I decided that one day I'd produce a lobster salad for lunch. It wasn't a success. What fancy restaurants were selling at top-dollar prices, ended up being tossed overboard – not one of my great culinary successes.

Berthed next to us in Kinsale was a vessel being used as a diving platform by a company that had bought the wreck of the *Lusitania*, an ocean liner that was sunk in May 1915 some eleven miles off the Old Head of Kinsale. The sinking of the *Lusitania* by a German U-boat and the loss of over 1,200 people contributed to the decision by the US to enter World War I in April 1917.

Of all my summer jobs being the relief cook on a fishing vessel was one of my most challenging and memorable.

CHAPTER 13

First Flight 1968

My first foreign trip alone was in 1968 when I went to London to work as a barman in my uncle's pub in Hounslow. I went to the USIT student travel office, which was then in a rundown building on Dame Street. I applied for a so-called USI Membership Card, which made be eligible for student discounts, and then booked a student charter flight from Dublin to Gatwick. The fare was £6.50 one-way, which was half the cost of a normal one-way ticket on Aer Lingus or British European Airways. It's funny how fate works; little did I know that I would later spend over fifteen years working for USIT.

The big day came, 12 June 1968, and I went out to the terminal building in Dublin Airport to check in for my flight to London Gatwick, operated by a British United Airways Viscount aircraft. I checked in, paid the 10-shilling airport tax and went upstairs to the departure gates in what is now the A Pier. Being anxious, I was one of the first to board and I sat down in the front row. It was only some years later that I learned that on a propeller-driven aeroplane it's less noisy in the rear.

Departure time came and went and there was much coming and going to and from the cockpit. Eventually a USIT representative came up the stairs into the cabin and said, 'You, and you – off.' Next minute I was on the tarmac watching the plane leave, with my baggage but without me.

The USIT representative booked me on the next Aer Lingus flight to Heathrow, which I remember cost £13. Flying to Heathrow Airport wasn't a problem because it was near Hounslow, where I'd be working; the only issue was that my bags had gone to Gatwick, about 70 km away. I took the Underground from Hounslow Central into central London and then a train down to Gatwick, where I collected my baggage. On the way back I took the Underground to Hounslow East, the nearest stop to The Tankerville Arms, where I was to work and stay for the summer.

When it was time for me to go home, I visited the USIT representative's

Student charter flight by BUA Viscount.

office in Victoria Street and booked my return flight from Gatwick. It was a beautiful day for flying and the view of the English countryside through the Viscount's large oval windows was magnificent.

As soon as I got home, I wrote a vitriolic letter to USIT to protest my overbooking (my first experience of that phenomenon) and received in response a two-page letter from Melissa Cannon, who later became a colleague and remains a friend to this day. It seems that the flight to Gatwick continued on to Rome, and the Dublin–Gatwick leg was overweight, so the simplest solution was to offload a couple of Gatwick-bound passengers.

CHAPTER 14

America, 1970

Planning

Coming up to Christmas 1969 I noticed USI Travel posters on the Student Representative Council notice board in the Trinity College entrance archway and in the Buttery Bar. 'Summer Jobs in America' was the headline, and underneath were the dates of charter flights to New York for £59 return. In those days most students needed to work for the summer to cover their fees or supplement living and travel expenses. Except of course for the students from Northern Ireland, who received generous financial support from the UK government. Many Northerners didn't need to go to America to earn their fees; their concern was mostly to repay debts incurred during infamous poker sessions in the Junior Common Room.

Between lectures, the talk was of going to America: where to go, when to go and which were the best jobs. The previous summer's Mecca had been Atlantic City, New Jersey.

According to second-year students, it was easy for girls to pick up waitressing or chamber maid jobs, while the lads were in demand as barmen, janitors or builders. I was told many made fortunes by holding down two jobs, living eight to a room and 'hot-bedding', i.e. a student working a night shift would use the same bed after it was vacated by a student with a day job.

The prophets of doom chirped up to say that the Irish had a bad reputation in Atlantic City because they were unreliable, leaving jobs at short notice because of better offers or in solidarity with a fellow Paddy who had incurred the wrath of the boss.

Cape Cod was hyped up by a second-year student who'd worked there the previous summer: 'A friend of mine has an uncle who owns an Irish pub in Hyannis. I'm sure he'll fix you up with a job.' That was the extent of the advance-planning strategy used by most of us.

If you stayed in the Buttery Bar for long enough, your head would be spinning with contradictory advice and filled with exotic place names such as Nantucket, the Catskills, Atlantic Beach and Cape May.

When to go was also a hot topic. Back then the J-1 student work visa was only valid from 1 June until 19 October. American students competing for summer jobs had the advantage of a head start, as their term ended in late May. On the other hand Irish students had the advantage of being able to stay right through till the Labor Day weekend in September, which traditionally marked the official end of the summer holidays in the US.

According to those in the know, you had to arrive in the States ready to start work by the Independence Day weekend in early July and stay till Labor Day, or at least tell your employer that you'd be staying.

To get a J-1 visa you needed to have either a definite job offer, proof of your own funds, together with an American relation to vouch for you, or have proof of a job interview. Not having a close relative in America or a definite job to go to, I had to rely on the latter. I was probably the only person in college who didn't have an uncle or cousin in America, so I had to find a potential employer willing to offer me a job interview.

In pre-internet, pre-Google days, it wasn't easy to get information on potential employers. The USIT office did have well-thumbed job directories compiled from questionnaires submitted by previous J-1ers. However, these were usually out of date, and employers rarely bothered to reply because they were inundated with job applications from Irish students. There was a sneaking suspicion that information on the best jobs never made it into the job directories but was passed like an inheritance to younger brothers and sisters.

Another source of information (albeit unfiltered) were the Yellow Pages classified phone directories that USI had in their offices in Harcourt Street. The first time I flicked through a weighty volume for New York City I couldn't believe the number of pages and classifications. The phonebooks were dogeared, and some pages had been torn out by previous readers too lazy to copy down contact details.

When I was in the USI office looking for advice, I told one of the staff there that I was thinking of going to Boston. She told me that one of her colleagues, Mary Ellen O' Driscoll, was from Boston and offered to have her speak with me. Mary Ellen was very helpful and gave me insider information on various areas of Boston, where to stay, and how to go about looking for a job.

Armed with a copy of the Hotels section of the Yellow Pages, I copied down the addresses of some properties in Boston. I posted out about twenty job applications to hotels and motels and waited anxiously for replies.

Three weeks passed and I hadn't received a single reply, but just as I was giving up hope, I arrived home to find a letter from the Red Roof Inn in the Boston suburb of Cambridge, offering to interview me when I arrived. This offer was sufficient to support my visa application and the following week I booked to fly out to New York on 16 June and started to count down the days.

The journey

In early June my tickets arrived, and shortly afterwards my passport came back from the American Embassy with the prized J-1 visa stamp. My departure day finally came, and my parents drove me to Dublin Airport. In the early 1970s there were no mobile phones or free calls via the internet, so I promised to write every week. Looking back, my parents seemed unperturbed at the sight of their only son heading off to America for a few months.

An ex-girlfriend's father, Billy Cuffe-Smith, was the captain on my flight, and I was invited to visit the cockpit during the transatlantic crossing from Shannon to JFK. The Boeing 707 was fully booked with 169 passengers and a crew of two pilots, a flight engineer and six air hostesses, as they were then known.

Arriving in New York

On arrival at JFK Airport, we were met by a USIT representative, who herded us onto coaches for the one-hour trip into midtown Manhattan. My first impression of New York was the stifling heat and sheer scale of the roads and buildings. Our destination was the Penn Garden Hotel located on the corner of 31st Street and 7th Avenue, almost opposite the famous Madison Square Garden arena. I'd never heard of it, but Americans who I met subsequently seemed impressed that my hotel was near such a well-known sports and entertainment venue.

The programme for arriving students involved a transfer from JFK Airport, a two-night stay in the hotel and a half-day orientation programme. The orientation programme was delivered by American students, who gave us information on the job situation, domestic travel, how to apply for a Social Security card, without which you couldn't legally be employed, and general information about living and working in America.

We were also given advice about finding somewhere to live and the vagaries of liquor laws that determined the minimum drinking age, which varied from state to state. There was an audible sigh of relief when we were told that in New York State the minimum age was eighteen, while in most neighbouring states it was twenty-one.

Onwards to Boston

I left the hotel after the orientation programme and walked to the Port Authority Bus Station on 42nd Street and 8th Avenue, where I bought a one-way Greyhound bus ticket to Boston. Having grown up with a primitive bus system in Ireland, I was surprised to find that there were departures every half hour between New York and cities such as Boston, Washington and Baltimore. I didn't have a reservation – in fact, it was impossible to make one; if the bus was full then extra buses were added so that nobody was left behind.

Even back in 1970 the bus journey to Boston was exclusively on a four-lane highway, part of Route 90 that ran along the east coast from Maine to Key West in Florida.

When I arrived in Boston, I negotiated the T transit system and made my way to the Red Roof Inn in Cambridge clutching the letter offering me a job interview. I was given a courteous interview but told that there were no longer any job vacancies. Looking back on it, I was very naïve to think that I could just arrive and get the first job that I applied for. It was by then late afternoon, and I needed somewhere to stay for a couple of days while I went job hunting. The guidebook that I had been given at the orientation included addresses of cheap hotels and hostels and I ended up staying at the YMCA in Boston South Station. It was not exactly salubrious, but it was cheap, centrally located and I had a private room; this was in the pre-Village People era.

The next morning, I went to the Government Center building and applied for my Social Security card. Armed with this, I went job hunting with a new sense of urgency, because my limited funds were already running low.

One of the places on my list was Boston Zoo, where I had seen jobs advertised in a local newspaper, but by the time I got there I was told there were no more vacancies. I was just leaving the office when a woman entered, introduced herself as the zoo veterinarian, heard my accent, and asked me about myself and what I was doing in America. This serendipitous encounter changed the course of my summer. She asked where I was staying, and when I told her, she said, 'Well you can't stay there. It's not safe; you must come and stay with myself and my husband. We'll drive down to South Station and collect your luggage.'

They lived in the Newton area, and after breakfast the next morning she explained that she did a regular natural history slot on children's TV and invited me along. She said that she first needed to go to the zoo, and I waited in the car. A few minutes I was surprised to see her returning with a tiny lion cub in here arms. She opened the passenger door and handed him to me. 'He's the guest on the TV show,' she explained. The cub was about the size of a large cat and seemed very content to sit on my lap during the drive to the studios in downtown Boston. Each time we stopped in traffic the drivers in the next lane did a double take when they saw the lion cub sitting in my lap. It was my first time in a TV studio, and I was fascinated by the whole set-up. Children in the audience were invited to pet the lion cub.

My fellow counsellors: Steve Masse (standing, 2nd right) and me (sitting, 1st right).

Camp Wing

Early next morning I heard a thud on the porch, which was the paperboy delivering the Sunday edition of the Boston Globe newspaper. I had never seen a paper with so many pages and specialist sections.

My host handed me the jobs section and I went through it line by line, taking note of Help Wanted job leads.

'What's a counsellor?' I asked. She explained that it involved supervising children in one of the many camps where children are sent during the summer holidays.

'This one is not too far from here, about thirty miles south of Boston on the way to Cape Cod, and they're looking for somebody to start right away. And it's for the whole summer. Why don't I call to see if you can go there for an interview?'

An hour or so later, we arrived in Camp Wing, near the small town of Duxbury, off Route 3, which links Boston to Cape Cod.

I got the job, said farewell to my benefactors and settled into cabin 13, where my job was to supervise a dozen or so seven- to ten-year-old boys from inner-city Boston. The camp comprised a dining room and log cabins among pine trees, with a small lake at the centre. The dining hall was situated in front of a parade ground with a tall flagpole, where every morning the campers stood to attention and recited the Pledge of Allegiance as the American flag was raised.

My title was general counsellor and there were also specialist camp counsellors who taught the children skills such as swimming, woodwork, painting and archery. The swim instructor was a gruff ex-Navy type who would shout, 'Eh, pull him out, John, he's a sinker,' each time one of the campers disappeared underwater.

General counsellors like me were responsible for the overall supervision of the children who were assigned to in their cabin. Each cabin was built of wide rough-sawn pine boards, about 30 ft long by 15 ft wide, with barracks style single beds for the campers and a small private cubicle at one end for the counsellor. The campers came for two-week sessions, but some stayed for two or more sessions. They were mostly from troubled backgrounds and lived in tough Boston neighbourhoods such as Dorchester and Charlestown. Bedwetting was commonplace, and mattresses were propped up against a tree to dry in the sun. I was given no training or police vetting and, as an only child, I had no experience of dealing with children, yet I was expected to supervise and act as a role model for these youngsters. My fellow counsellors were mostly Americans from the local area (many of them were ex-campers) and a handful of English and Scots were there as part of the BUNACAMP or Camp America programmes.

Like other camps, Camp Wing closed at the end of August, and while I really enjoyed my time there, I barely made enough money to cover my airfare, and certainly not enough to travel around the States as I had planned. I had no alternative but to cut short my visit and return home in the first week of September.

I was the counsellor in charge of Cabin 13.

I got a unique insight into the real America and made many friends, one of whom, Steve Masse, a fellow counsellor, has visited me in Ireland and remains a close friend fifty years later. In April 2010 I met up with Steve in Boston and we drove down to Cape Wing to find that the place looked very much the same, except that the buildings and cabins looked smaller than we'd remembered.

I've never forgotten the kindness that I was shown by strangers during my J-1 adventure. Americans are too often portrayed in a negative way, but during my many trips to the US over the years I have also seen the warm, generous side of so-called ordinary Americans.

The summer of 1970 was the start of my love affair with America, and it didn't wane until the neo-conservatives and evangelical Christian right began to dominate and divide American society.

CHAPTER 15

Summer in New York, 1974

Jackie and I were married in September 1973 and for the next ten months we lived with Jackie's parents in the Clonskeagh suburb of Dublin, before moving into a rented house. The overriding objective was to buy a house, the first step of which was to save a 10 per cent deposit. Depending on the neighbourhood, prices ranged from £6,500 to £13,000 for a three-bedroom semi-detached house. In calculating mortgage amounts, banks would only consider one salary per couple and mortgages were limited to 2.5 times salary. However, most employers would bend the rules and declare an inflated salary.

I am blessed with serendipity, and this time it came when I was given the opportunity to manage the USIT office in New York for the June–October period, when over 7,000 Irish students were expected to travel to the US for summer jobs. Jackie gave up her job in Irish Pensions Trust, and at the end of May 1974 we flew to New York to set up the office and make hotel arrangements for the Irish invasion.

Our base that year was the Hotel Wellington on the corner of 7th Avenue and 55th Street – a super location near Carnegie Hall and Central Park South. We had a complimentary two-bedroom suite, which we shared with a colleague, Mary Boyd.

Meeting and greeting
My almost daily routine for the month of June and early July involved taking the Carey Airport Bus from the East Side Air Terminal to JFK, where I'd wait near the Aer Lingus desk in the International Arrivals building.

J-1 participants were mostly first-year undergraduates aged nineteen to twenty, the majority of whom had never been outside of Ireland. The combination of a seven-hour flight with free booze, jet lag, 30°C heat, high humidity and the hustle and noise of Manhattan was a shock to their systems.

Irish students were instantly recognisable – they were the pale and slightly shell-shocked passengers emerging from the customs hall. I'd direct them to waiting charter buses: 'Out the door, cross the street, right and follow the sign for area D.' When I had rounded up the last stragglers, I'd board the first bus and the convoy of three to four buses would head for Manhattan. The route usually involved using the Midtown Tunnel and there were always gasps of surprise at the first glimpse of the Manhattan skyline. When the students arrived at the hotel, we would hand out keys to pre-allocated twin-bedded rooms.

When they unpacked, the braver souls headed out in small groups to explore the neighbourhood, have a drink and get something to eat. It wasn't long before they discovered a nearby Burger 'n' Brew restaurant, which offered unlimited beer with each meal. Anecdotal feedback was that the restaurant discouraged Irish students from overstaying their welcome by turning off the air conditioning.

Breakfast was organised by Virginia, a formidable Greek woman who ran the coffee shop/diner in the Wellington Hotel. She was very appreciative of our business and always insisted on picking up the tab when Jackie or I ate there.

The Hotel Wellington on the corner of 7th Avenue and 55th Street, our New York base in 1974.

In early August exam results were published and we were busy changing flight reservations for students who had to return to Ireland earlier than planned to resit exams. A sizeable number only spent a few days at home and then came back to America to work till the end of the summer. There were also a small number of students who flew home for long weekends to play an important match for their GAA club.

Eastbound exodus

My routine changed in September with the first of the eastbound charters from JFK to Shannon and Dublin. The departures were always in the evening, and once more I was trekking out to JFK, this time to the Aer Lingus terminal in the East Wing, where I was available to issue last-minute tickets and sort out any overbookings. I noticed a change the departing students – whereas they had arrived pale faced and apprehensive, they were leaving sun-kissed and self-confident. Unbeknownst to me at the time, one of the Aer Lingus duty managers, Derek O'Brien, became a colleague of mine in Ryanair over a decade later.

Going on the J-1 programme has been a rite of passage for Irish students for over five decades and long may it continue.

Old International Arrivals Building (IAB) with Aer Lingus B707 in the foreground.

CHAPTER 16

Bangkok Quickie, 1976

In 1976 I was working in USIT as marketing manager and became mates with Peter Hicks, the manager of the Australian student travel organisation's (AUSTS) London office on Euston Road. Peter rather unkindly described it as a handholding, bum-wiping centre for the thousands of young Aussies who travelled to Britain on their big OE – big overseas experience.

These were pre-internet days and the AUSTS office was the umbilical cord between Australia and London. The staff acted as agony aunts and the office canteen fridge was full of jars of Vegemite and tins of Foster's beer that arrived on a regular basis, courtesy of the Qantas Airways station manager at Heathrow. Those were the days before anyone of had even heard of Foster's, never mind tasted it.

I thought that Peter's management style was rather brash, but in hindsight he was simply being an Aussie.

One night in Bangkok
Monday 22 February 1976 was a bleak, cold day. I was sitting in my office in Dublin when I got a call from Peter. He was typically brisk and to the point: 'How do you fancy a free trip to Bangkok, mate?' to which I gave a cautious response, because with Peter you just never quite knew what he might have in mind. He proceeded to rattle off the itinerary. I was to make my own way to London the next morning and meet him at Gatwick, where we'd take a charter flight to Copenhagen and then an overnight charter flight to Bangkok. We would arrive in Bangkok late in the afternoon of 24 February and leave the next evening, 25 February and be back in Copenhagen early in the morning of 26 February. A real quickie. Because all the flights had plenty of empty seats, we travelled on free staff tickets.

I remember being very excited at the time about a trip to Thailand, my first long-haul trip, but now the thought of all that travelling to spend less than twenty-four hours in Bangkok sounds like pure hell. This was basic economy-class travel without in-flight movies or comfy business-class seats.

I met Peter in Gatwick Airport, by which time a long queue had formed at the check-in desk for our Sterling Airways charter flight to Copenhagen. I walked to join the end of the queue, but Peter grabbed my arm and marched us to the front of the line.

'Don't mind those dopey Poms,' he said. 'They'd queue to catch a bloody cold.'

We arrived in Copenhagen and checked in for our Maersk Air Boeing 720 charter flight to Bangkok, which took off about 8 p.m. After dinner the cabin lights were dimmed, and we tried to get some sleep. In the middle of the night, I woke up and opened the window blind and saw hundreds of fires that looked like candles twinkling on what was an otherwise black landscape below. We were flying over the Middle East and what I was seeing for the first time were the routine burn-offs of a major oil field.

Shortly after dawn we touched down at Abu Dhabi, where the aircraft refuelled. During the short stopover Peter and I enjoyed a cold beer looking out at the sand dunes just beyond the airport perimeter. At the time I didn't think about the significance of drinking alcohol in a Muslim country.

En route to Bangkok – how did I end up in the middle seat?

When we began our descent into Bangkok's Don Mueang Airport and broke through the cloud I got my first glimpse of paddy fields, small villages and exotic vegetation. When the aircraft doors were opened, I was hit by a torrent of hot, humid air and a heady cocktail of smells. It was amazing to think that only yesterday I'd left the depths of the northern European winter and now I was in Thailand walking across the tarmac in my shirtsleeves.

Real Thai food

Waiting for us in the arrivals hall was Suzy Barry, Peter's colleague who headed up the Australian student travel office in Bangkok. By coincidence, some of my colleagues from USIT had just arrived in Bangkok on their way back from Australia, so we went straight from the airport to a restaurant, where Suzy and the local staff guided us through the menu. I have always been an adventurous eater, but I had never tasted anything like Thai food. The flavour combinations of lemongrass, coriander, fish sauce, etc. were fantastic, and to this day I love Thai food. It's a pity that so many restaurants are serving poor-quality food and calling it Thai. There are of course excellent Thai restaurants around, and one of my favourites was the Blue Elephant in Paris or London.

Eventually the cocktail of jet lag, lack of sleep, good food and Singha beer took over and I headed back to the Vieng Tai Hotel, checked in, and fell into bed.

Bangkok experiences

I awoke slowly from a deep sleep and gradually became aware of my surroundings. For a moment or two I was confused as to where I was but then everything slotted into place – I was in Bangkok. My bedroom was on the second floor of the hotel, looking out over a lane and one of Bangkok's numerous klongs, or canals. It was just before 7 a.m. and the sun was streaming through the thin curtains. I got out of bed and opened the window. Just below me the lane was packed with people and animals; the smoke from small cooking stoves mixed with a predawn mist to create a slightly ethereal scene. Buddhist monks, some of them just boys, wandered among the crowds with begging bowls, hoping for donations of food and money. Nearly 95 per cent of Thailand's population is Buddhist and it is common for young men to serve as monks for a few years before returning to secular life.

Floating markets

After breakfast, Peter and I joined a small group of backpackers on a boat trip along the klongs to one of Bangkok's many floating markets. We were driven in a minibus through the city's chaotic, noisy streets, weaving our way past cars, trucks and tuk-tuks – noisy motorised rickshaws powered by moped engines. When we arrived at a small pier, we boarded a narrow boat with a distinctive long-tail engine – basically a car engine with a propeller shaft attached, which sped through the narrow canals, barely missing other boats.

I am sure that the people who design scary amusement-park rides take inspiration from high-speed boat trips in Bangkok.

After about fifteen minutes we left the main canal system and headed into a labyrinth of narrower waterways lined with traditional teak houses and shacks built precariously on stilts over the water. By now the sun was up and people were starting their daily chores. The canals are an integral part of daily life; we saw women waist deep washing clothes; animals drinking; teeth being brushed and even the occasional dead dog floating in the rushes.

The floating market was filled with dozens of small, narrow boats crammed together and overflowing with fresh produce. The display was incredible – rows of different-coloured chillies contrasted with all the different hues of green of the coriander, pak choi, basil and mint. In Ireland in the mid-seventies a humble aubergine was considered exotic. The market traders were almost exclusively women, who constantly jockeyed for position, getting their craft as close as possible to the shoppers in other boats.

Leaving the floating market, we were driven to a jewellery shop owed by our tour guide's brother. At the time I was naïve and didn't realise that every tour guide had a brother or cousin who owed a shop selling jade, jewellery or tacky souvenirs, and a visit was almost a mandatory part of the tour. I was tempted and bought an emerald ring for Jackie, which cost £60 – the equivalent of a week's salary. Jackie liked the ring, and when she had it valued in Dublin it turned out that I had made a good buy.

Because of the risk of cholera, it's not surprising that many of klongs have been drained and filled. There are still some floating markets, but they are largely commercialised photo opportunities. Back then it was still an authentic part of everyday life and commerce in Bangkok.

The Bangkok Chair

The final stop of the tour was an outdoor market that had stalls selling rattan and wooden furniture. I spotted a rattan baby chair with wheels, which I thought would be the perfect gift for my young daughter, Elaine. It was beautifully made and a bargain, but no sooner had I handed over the money than Peter said, 'That's lovely, mate, but now you've got to get it home.' I had a moment of buyers regret but I dismissed the problem and carried the baby chair back to the hotel.

Before going back to the airport for our return flight, we went out to dinner, and I was introduced to Mekhong, the infamous rice-based Thai whiskey. The only similarity with our whiskey is its brown colour and high alcohol content. It's not unlike rum and slips down easier when mixed with coke. In Ireland and Scotland, premium whiskey brands are matured for ten or twenty years, but not so with Mekhong. Turn over a bottle of Mekhong and the date that's printed on the back of label is a best-before date, usually no more than a few weeks later.

Getting home

The Maersk Air cabin crew had also overnighted in Bangkok, and they were surprised to see some familiar faces on the return leg. We landed in Copenhagen the next morning in the middle of a snowstorm, feeling seedy after the long flight, very little sleep and the afterburn of Mekhong.

My connecting flight to Dublin was cancelled, and I was forced to spend the night in Copenhagen before flying home the following day. The baby chair didn't arrive on the same flight, but when it was delivered it was a big hit with Elaine. It became known as the Bangkok Chair and was around for many years, till eventually the wheels fell off and the rattan unravelled.

Elaine in her Bangkok Chair.

CHAPTER 17

¡Viva Cuba!

During the late 1970s, in addition to my job in USIT, I was appointed the part-time project manager for the International Student Travel Conference (ISTC), which acted as an umbrella organisation for the fifty-plus Student Travel Bureau around the world. Cold War politics was mirrored in the international student travel community – the ISTC had begun life as the ISC, a CIA surrogate based in Leiden in the Netherlands. At the same time the International Union of Students (IUS) was set up in Prague with more than a little help from the Kremlin. By the late 1960s the ISTC was a legitimate travel organisation, but it's politics and committees still reflected East–West politics.

World Festival of Youth and Students
The 11th World Festival of Youth and Students, organised by the IUS, was held in Cuba in July 1978. It was more of a party-political conference than a festival in the real sense of the word. Over 18,000 participants were eligible to attend, but only those of the right hue, a deep shade of pink, were invited.

The IUS considered the ISTC to be a 'fraternal organisation' and invited it to send a small delegation to attend the festival. Because part of the festival programme was a student travel fair, it was agreed that I would travel to Cuba to represent the ISTC.

Schlepping to Havana
In 1978 getting from Dublin to Havana with a heavy portable display stand was not as easy as it might be today. Cubana, the Cuban national airline did not offer transatlantic services, nor were there charter flights from Europe. The 'portable' display was in reality not very portable at all. True, the six panels did fit into a carrying case, but the overall weight and the awkward size meant that it was only portable in that it could be carried by two strong men with abnormally long arms.

Armed with a briefcase, suitcase and the display stand, I began my Cuban odyssey. The first leg was simple, I flew on Aer Lingus from Dublin to JFK. After that the real odyssey began. My suitcase arrived but there was no sign of the display case on the conveyor bel. It was soon recovered at the 'out of gauge' collection point, however. Next came the job of clearing US Customs and telling a little white lie about my destination, which I said was Montreal. I felt that declaring I was bound for Havana might not be a smart move.

I finally made it outside the International Arrivals building in JFK and my next task was to find a taxi to take me and my baggage the ten miles to La Guardia Airport for my flight to Montreal. In those days taxis in New York came in two varieties and I needed a Checker, a large square-shaped taxi that could accommodate my outsized load. By the time I got to La Guardia, I was soaked in perspiration and looked forward to sitting in the air-conditioned terminal to wait for my Air Canada flight to Montreal.

I always found Canadian Customs to be quite intimidating; it was one of the few places where you needed to complete a customs declaration form. The arrival of an Irishman with a large display stand and a story about going to Cuba made the day of a bored customs official in Montreal. My marathon journey continued with a taxi ride from Dorval Airport to the new international airport about thirty-five miles north in Mirabel. The new airport was an attempt by the Canadian government to force airlines to fly there rather than the more convenient airport in Dorval. Finally, market forces prevailed and in the mid-1990s airlines were once again allowed back to Dorval, and Mirabel became hub for cargo airlines and occasional charter flights.

By the time I got to Mirabel it was about 6 p.m. and I'd been travelling for the best part of twelve hours that day. But I still had one more flight to go – a six-hour flight to Havana on an IL-62 operated by the Cuban state airline – Cubana, which was due to leave Montreal at 11.30 p.m. that night.

I spent the long layover in the almost empty modern terminal building, but finally it was time to board the Plane Mate vehicle that took passengers from the terminal building to their flight.

After leaving Canadian airspace, Cubana flights were required to detour over the ocean to avoid US airspace.

Havana

I arrived in Havana in the early morning of 30 July and arranged a taxi to take me to my hotel in the centre of the city; it was great to have a shower and take a nap in an air-conditioned bedroom. My sleep was interrupted by a key turning in the door and the noisy arrival of my roommate, Mongi Baklouti, the director of the Tunisian student travel organisation.

As it was by now coming up to lunch time, we headed down to the hotel restaurant. I ordered a beer and asked Mongi what he'd like to drink.

'Are we more than 1,000 km from Tunis?' he whispered.

'Sure, why are you asking?'

'It means I am a traveller, and this means I can drink alcohol.' Sounding very relived, he said, 'A beer, please.'

The next day I needed to get the display stand to the International Youth Festival venue and erect it in the lobby area. That was a major logistical exercise in 35-degree heat and 90 per cent humidity, but it was made easier by the promise of a cold Spanish beer at the end of the day.

Architecturally Havana looked very much the same as in the 1950s, when Fidel Castro overthrew the Batista regime. One of the most visible signs of the US embargo were the iconic 1950s American cars that had been lovingly maintained over the years. What will happen to these wonderful old cars when the US embargo is eventually lifted? Let's hope they won't be scrapped in favour of bland-looking Japanese and Korean imports.

One evening I was invited to a party at the local university on the outskirts of Havana, attended by other 'fraternal student delegations' from around the world. I met the Irish group from the Union of Students in Ireland as well as assorted communist and socialist organisations from the UK and Ireland, some of which I'd never heard of; they were probably hastily formed to take advantage of a subsidised trip to the sun.

The party was a BBQ in the gardens of the university and involved copious amounts of Cuba libres, singing and dancing. By about midnight I was in flying form, and soon after I was poured into a taxi and dispatched back to the hotel. My knowledge of Spanish is limited to essential phrases such as the ordering of two beers (I never mastered ordering just one), asking for a restaurant bill and getting directions to the toilet. However, on that taxi ride back into Havana I had a 'speaking in tongues' experience and chattered nonstop to the driver in what I thought was Spanish, but in hindsight was probably complete drivel. I may have put a strain on Irish–Cuban relations for decades to come.

When eventually I got back to my hotel room, I collapsed onto the bed and fell into a deep sleep. The next morning, I woke up with a terrible hangover.

My roommate, Mongi, tried his best to describe my appearance the previous night: 'You were like a tortoise, lying on your back with four limbs in the air.' Oh dear.

Cruise ship lunch

Later in the week I was part of a small delegation that was invited to have lunch on a Russian cruise ship, the Shota Rustaveli, which was anchored in Havana Harbour, having just arrived with half of the large Soviet delegation.

The Shota Rustaveli brought the USSR delegations to Havana.

The first group would fly home and the second group would go back by sea. A tender brought us out to the ship and we were ushered into a spacious stateroom on one of the upper decks, with great views of the busy harbour and the city in the background.

The stateroom was air-conditioned, and it was like stepping into a refrigerator. After a brief tour of the ship, we were subjected to a fifteen-minute monologue of fraternal greetings from the youth of the Soviet Union, delivered by the ship's political cadre and translated by a young man named Alexander Pasekunov, a paid-up, card-carrying member of Komsomol, the youth wing of the Communist Party of the Soviet Union.

By an amazing coincidence I met Alexander (Sasha) again in Ukraine in 1992, when I was part of the team setting up Ukraine International Airlines (UIA). He was the interpreter working for our client, Guinness Peat Aviation, and was assigned to work with the Irish team setting up UIA. We worked there together for over year before we discovered that we'd met briefly in Cuba almost fifteen years previously.

Fidel Castro

Towards the end of the festival, the delegates were bused into the main square in Havana, where we were forced to stand in the blazing sun and listen to Fidel Castro deliver one of his famous two-hour speeches.

There was no translation, but a couple of English-speaking Cubans provided me with an occasional summaries. The topics were predictable: the role of youth in the pursuit of world peace and the injustices of the US embargo. The speech was interspersed with applause, which I thought meant that that it was finally over, and we could escape. But every very time I thought it was ending, Castro would take the applause as a signal that we wanted more. He became reenergised and continued his diatribe on the evils of world capitalism, its multi-faceted running dogs and their lackeys.

Eventually there was a longer period of applause and Castro waved to the crowd before proceeding to embrace every one of the many assembled dignitaries on the podium.

When I eventually got back to the hotel, I was greeted excitedly by our head of delegation, Ursi Silberschmidt, a Swiss colleague. 'Fidel kissed me on the cheek!' she declared pointing to her left cheek. 'I'm not going to wash for a week!' I didn't share her enthusiasm and grumbled about having to stand in the sun and listen to the political meanderings of her newfound hero.

Escape

The display stand that I had brought from Dublin was used at the student travel fair, and although it was very poorly attended, I had to stay to the bitter end. By pulling a few strings I managed to get myself on an Air Canada charter flight to Montreal and from there directly back to Dublin on the twice-weekly Aer Lingus flight. This was a lucky break on several fronts in that I was able to leave the display stand behind, to be transported back to Zürich by courier, and I didn't have to endure the 'delights' of another flight on Cubana. As a bonus I saw the Northern Lights on the flight from Montreal to Dublin.

Since Castro came to power the Cuban-American community in Miami and America's paranoia around communism have meant that the island has been isolated for decades. That changed in the 1990s when Canada, Spain and several European countries began investing in the tourism infrastructure, and Europeans and Canadians began visiting Cuba in increasing numbers.

CHAPTER 18

Flying on Concorde, 1983

Because there was a shortage of capacity on scheduled flights in high season, USIT operated summertime charter flights from Dublin and London to Athens. In pre-euro times, Greece, like every other member state, had its own national currency, the drachma, and there were strict restrictions on the amount of foreign currency that could be taken out of Greece. By the end of the summer, the USIT office in Athens was awash with drachma and it was proving time-consuming and difficult to repatriate them and convert them to Irish punts. One possible solution was to use the drachma to pay the charter airline's refuelling bills in Athens, but that required Gordon Colleary and myself going to Athens to negotiate with the fuel supplier and central bank.

On our second day there, Gordon got a call from his secretary in Dublin to say that the US State Department had finally agreed to a meeting with the Irish Embassy to discuss the future of the J-1 visa programme, and a plan to dramatically cut the allocation for Ireland. The meeting was to take place in Washington the next afternoon, and USIT was invited to join the Irish delegation.

Cunning plan
It was already mid-morning in Athens, so how could we possibly get to Washington by the next morning? Gordon always travelled with the pocket edition of the Official Airline Guide (OAG) and within minutes he had figured out a routing to get us to Washington by late that night. Gordon's plan involved using drachma to buy two first-class return tickets from Athens to Washington via Zürich and London. The cunning part was for us to only use the tickets one way to Washington and to send the unused portion of the tickets to the British Airways office in Dublin for a refund in Irish punts. It was killing two birds with one stone; we would get to Washington for the meeting and we would circumvent the Greek exchange control regulations.

I was sent to the British Airways office in Syntagma Square with a briefcase full of drachmas to pay for the tickets. The agent in the BA office was gobsmacked by my request to upgrade to Concorde for the Heathrow to JFK leg. When I told him that we needed to be on the Swissair flight to Zürich that afternoon, he nearly had a meltdown, but the seats were confirmed. So far, so good.

While I was organising the tickets, Gordon bought a couple of carry-on bags, into which we packed some toiletries and a change of clothes from our suitcases. Then we hopped into a taxi for the airport, which was then very close to the city.

Tight connections

Because we had only cabin baggage, we were able to make the short connection in Zürich onto a British Airways flight to Heathrow. There were air-traffic delays and by the time we reached the parking stand in Heathrow, it was less than an hour before the Concorde would depart for JFK.

As we disembarked from the British Airways flight, a ramp agent ushered us onto a minibus, and we were driven across the ramp directly to the Concorde Lounge. We were checked in and handed a glass of champagne, which we had to gulp down as soon as the boarding call was made. It seems unreal now that we were able to board without any security checks, but they were different times.

My boarding pass was for seat 23A on BA003 departing at 19.30 and due to arrive in JFK around three and a half hours later at 18.25 (local time).

Take-off

Take-off was amazing – the noise and acceleration were tremendous. The captain had already warned us that approximately four minutes after take-off there would be a 'falling' sensation as the afterburners were turned off. He was right. Once we had cleared the British coast over the Bristol Channel, the afterburners were again engaged and we climbed towards 50,000 ft and accelerated to our cruising speed of Mach 2, twice the speed of sound, approximately 2,180 km/h.

After all that excitement we settled back to enjoy the unique Concorde experience. The cabin was narrow compared to normal subsonic aircraft, and the windows were tiny – about the size of small saucer. The seats were business class, four across.

Because the aircraft capacity was only 100 seats, the service was very personal. Wine and champagne were poured from full bottles carried in a specially designed wicker basket, and meals were served on Royal Doulton china.

We looked around at our fellow passengers to see if we recognised any celebrities. While there were a few 'suits', most of our fellow passengers were young men – some very casually dressed. We speculated that they might be pop stars – it was a decade or so before the dot-com boom. We later learned that they were 'on-board couriers' carrying original legal documents, which had been signed that afternoon in London and would be countersigned that evening in New York. The courier would then hop on the last BA overnight subsonic flight back to London.

We landed in JFK on time and taxied to the dedicated Concorde immigration and customs facility. Because we had only cabin bags, within about thirty minutes, we were in a cab to La Guardia Airport and on the last leg of our journey to Washington. Having breakfast in Athens that morning I had no idea that I'd be having a nightcap in a hotel in Washington DC.

The postscript to the story was that the J-1 visa programme was saved (albeit with reduced numbers), but British Airways insisted that the refund be processed by their office in Athens and that the refund would be in … drachma.

CHAPTER 19

Aruba, 1990/91

CHL Consulting had several EU-funded projects, including the development of a tourist master plan for the Dutch Caribbean island of Aruba. I was asked to examine the air access aspect of the plan, which involved spending some time with a team of Costa Ricans who were managing the airline.

My first trip to Aruba was in November 1990, when I travelled there with Philip Heneghan; I returned in 1991 on a consultancy project for Air Aruba. At the time the airline was expanding into the lucrative US market, offering flights from Miami and Newark. Aruba, the most commercialised of the Dutch Leeward Islands, was popular with American tourists because, unlike other parts of the Caribbean, the Leeward Islands were outside the hurricane belt.

I enjoyed my trips to Aruba, where I stayed at a resort hotel on the beach. It always felt weird arriving back from the office in jacket and tie when all the other guests were in swimming costumes or beach wear, sipping cocktails at the pool bar. Like most hotels in Aruba, mine had a casino, and once or twice a week I'd join a table of American guests to play blackjack. My rule was to buy $100 of chips and play until I'd either lost them all or I was up more than $50. The drinks were free, and my fellow gamblers were good fun and didn't take the game too seriously.

One of my tasks was to review the Air Aruba customer service and to visit the airline's sales office in Miami. I flew to Miami on an Air Aruba flight operated by a Boeing 757 on lease from Cardiff-based Inter European Airways. Most of the three-hour-and-fifteen-minute flight was over the beautiful blue Caribbean, which I saw from the jump seat in the cockpit. Just over an hour into the flight, the pilots pointed out a land mass directly ahead – Hispaniola, the second-largest island of the West Indies, divided into the Republic of Haiti and the Dominican Republic. The border between the two countries was clearly visible from the air. Haiti looked dry and impoverished compared to the relative green of the Dominican Republic.

Chapter 20

Italia 90

Everyone's an expert

The World Cup held in Italy in summer 1990 created a feel-good umbrella that impacted on all aspects of Irish life. For the first time in history the Republic of Ireland made it to the finals of the World Cup. Almost overnight everyone became a soccer fan – grannies, GAA folk, rugby fans and the dogs on the street all became experts on the off-side rule and booed when an opposition player took a dive. The chant of 'Olé, Olé, Olé' erupted spontaneously at almost every social occasion.

As Ireland progressed through the competition, we all wanted to be part of a journey that might just end with winning the World Cup. The country was in the grip of World Cup fever and hardcore soccer fans started an exodus to Italy. There were stories told of enterprising Irish fans travelling to Italy by obscure routes and modes of transport. One of my favourites was of a supporter from Finglas who told his wife that he was 'going out to get a pint of milk' and returned home three weeks later. It seems that he and a few fellas drove a minibus the 2,000 km to Italy and stayed in campsites along the way.

Sports Tours

My involvement with Italia 90 began when USIT decided to operate a charter-flight programme to get the fans to games in Italy. Hotel beds near the venues were either fully booked or exorbitantly priced, so we decided to offer 'day trips' from Dublin that would include a return flight, coach transfer from the airport to the ground and back and optional match tickets. This programme was branded Sports Tours, and I managed it out of the USIT/Eurotrain office in Middle Abbey Street.

The most challenging part was getting the match tickets. A colleague had to do some dubious deals with some even more dubious characters in Switzerland.

Ireland v England

The first trip was for the Ireland v England game in Cagliari on 11 June 1990 at 9 p.m. We chartered a Boeing 727 from Europe Aéro Service based in Perpignan, scheduled to leave Dublin at lunch time, wait on the ground in Cagliari until just after midnight and then fly back to Dublin. I went to Dublin Airport to oversee the check-in and boarding, all of which went smoothly. The last passengers were boarded when the Aer Lingus red cap (dispatcher) asked if I was travelling. I hesitated for a minute, and he said, 'Let me have a word with the skipper and see if he'll take you on the jump seat.'

Ten minutes later we were airborne, with me sitting in the cockpit and Jackie getting a phone call from the red cap telling her I wouldn't be home for dinner.

I unexpectedly attended my very first soccer game in Sardinia in a business suit! The result was a 1–1 draw, which kept Ireland's hopes alive.

Ireland v Netherlands

Our next operation was for the Ireland v Netherlands game on 21 June 1990 in Palermo, another 9 p.m. kick-off. For this trip we chartered a British Airtours Boeing 757 and arrived in Palermo late in the afternoon, where coaches were waiting to transfer fans directly to the Stadio La Favorita. On this flight we had several VIPs, including Mr Liam Hamilton, the chief justice of Ireland, a friend of Gordon Colleary's, who also travelled.

The game again ended in a 1–1 draw, and afterwards the Irish fans boarded coaches for a short transfer to the restaurant we'd booked for dinner. The idea was to stay there till 2 a.m. before going back to the airport for the flight home.

The Italian authorities were paranoid about soccer hooligans and possible clashes between Irish and Dutch fans. While their fears were unfounded, they still enforced an embargo on selling or serving alcohol before midnight, including at the restaurant we'd booked for the after-match dinner.

There was almost a revolt when the hardcore Dubs were told by the waiters that there would be no alcohol until midnight. I noticed Gordon whispering something to our Italian tour guide, who nodded and disappeared out of the restaurant. About fifteen minutes later he returned with a small group of senior carabinieri and the harbour master in full dress uniform, feathered hats, and all. They were introduced to the chief justice and accepted Gordon's invitation to stay for dinner. The senior carabinieri officer had words with the restaurant manager, who in turn spoke to the head waiter, and within minutes large bottles of cold beer were placed on every table – Gordon was the hero of the moment. One fan was overheard saying, 'Fair dos, head.'

We left the restaurant in the early hours and headed back to the airport. The aircraft was fuelled and ready to go and we took off just as the sun started to rise in the east. A good result all round.

Shoot-out with Romania

Because all three of Ireland's group games had ended in a draw, the result of a knockout game against Romania on 25 June would determine if Ireland would progress to the quarter finals or go home. It seemed the whole country was watching the game, which ended with the sides drawn 0–0, meaning a penalty shoot-out would determine the result. The save by the Irish goalkeeper Packie Bonner and the successful shot by Dave O'Leary resulted in screaming and hollering in every Irish pub and house in the country. We were off to Rome!

Ireland v Italy

Our quarter final opponents were Italy, and the game was to be played in the Stadio Olimpico in Rome at 9 p.m. on 30 June 1990.

Demand for aircraft was such that planes were being sourced from all over Europe, with charter prices reflecting the costs of positioning empty aircraft from the airline's home base to and from Dublin. Sports Tours decided to offer a one-night package, including return flight, hotel and match tickets. Our charter broker eventually sourced a Boeing 737 from Norwegian operator Busy Bee to operate the Dublin to Rome leg and Air Europe for the inbound flight from Rome to Dublin the next day. I didn't really want to tell the fans that the airline was called Busy Bee, so when asked, I said it was a 'Norwegian airline'.

Sales started strongly but the day before departure we had twenty empty seats that were sold at cost price to family and friends. The whole Dawson clan took off for Rome! My daughter Amy was ten and Elaine was fifteen and they had serious bragging rights about going to Rome and were the envy of their schoolmates.

Oslo based Busy Bee Airlines flew Irish fans to Rome.

The Busy Bee aircraft arrived from Oslo, and over a hundred excited Irish fans were gathered in the gate area. As the large cartoon drawing of a bee on the aircraft tail became visible, the good-humoured crowd began chanting 'Busy Bee, Busy Bee, Busy Bee' to the tune of a football anthem.

The passengers were a cross-section of Irish society, including singer Chris de Burgh and some of his friends, who had planned to use a private jet to get to Rome. However, there were no landing slots in Rome Ciampino Airport, so they had to buy tickets on our flight.

The atmosphere in the Olympic Stadium was amazing. The Irish and Italian fans were in good spirits and the singing and chanting never stopped. Except that is until Salvatore Schillaci broke Irish hearts with a match-winning goal in the thirty-eighth minute.

At the end of the game the Irish fans cheered and cheered and stayed on to celebrate long after the Italian fans had gone home – the Taoiseach of the day, Charles Haughey, even joined in the lap of honour. It was as if we had won the World Cup.

Payload problems

The return to Dublin was no less dramatic. All the passengers were on board the Air Europe aircraft ready for a mid-afternoon departure, but because of the high temperature and the short runway at Rome Ciampino Airport, there were payload restrictions, i.e. the aircraft was too heavy to take off for a three-hour flight. As I was the charterer, the captain gave me two choices, either stop en route to refuel (at USIT's expense) or offload twenty passengers. The decision was easy when he added that he'd spoken to the captain of a Balair flight also heading to Dublin, who had agreed to take the surplus passengers. I discreetly spoke to the staff passengers, including my family, and asked them to disembark. The fact that nobody had checked in baggage meant that we were escorted across the apron to the nearby Balair MD-83 aircraft. This aircraft also had payload issues, which meant we had to make a refuelling stop in Basel, but we were so grateful to be getting home that there weren't many complaints.

Patricia the Stripper

I learned later that passengers on the Air Europe flight were entertained by Chris de Burgh, who used the aircraft PA sound system to belt out a rendition of 'Patricia the Stripper'. The cabin crew joined in the fun and animated the lyrics by throwing items of underwear from their overnight kit bags over the curtain at the front of the cabin – real in-flight entertainment. My family have never forgiven me.

CHAPTER 21

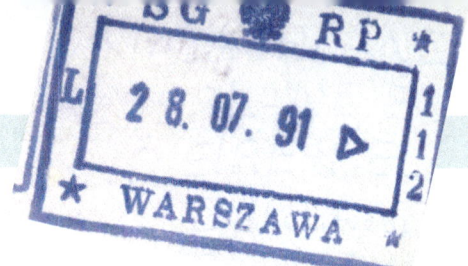

LOT Polish Airlines, 1991

In 1991 the Polish government passed a law to privatise the national carrier, LOT, and in 1992 it became a company wholly owned by the Polish State Treasury. The airline engaged IDI Ireland to assist in the privatisation and modernisation process, and I was part of a small team of ex-Ryanair managers who spent some time in Warsaw reviewing the main departmental functions, including finance, commercial, maintenance, engineering and flight operations.

Because my focus was on the commercial section of the report, I arranged to meet the commercial department team to discuss their route-planning strategy and to probe deeper into the rationale for operating certain routes. LOT had very few international flights and I was curious why there were flights from Warsaw to both Lyon and Geneva, given that the two cities are less than 100 km apart. There was an awkward silence but eventually one of the more senior managers explained that a previous chairman had a romantic liaison with a woman in Lyon – definitely a niche route.

I also interviewed the charter manager and asked about the cluster of flights departing from Dubai to Warsaw every weekend. Why were two to three flights departing within ten minutes of each other? He explained this was because senior pilots were not only entitled to free flights for themselves

LOT Polish Airlines TU-154 jet; modelled on B727

and their families, but they also had almost unlimited free baggage allowance. White goods like refrigerators and washing machines were expensive in Poland but were significantly cheaper in Dubai. Some pilots got into the informal import business; they would by fly to Dubai for free, purchase the goods, then check them in as personal baggage.

However, there was never enough room for all the 'baggage', so it was loaded onto a second flight, which departed immediately after the previous flight. On arrival in Warsaw, the 'baggage' was placed on the passenger baggage belts because theft was rife in the cargo warehouse and customs officials were easily bribed. Understandably we recommended fundamental changes to so-called privilege travel benefits.

We were based at the LOT head office in the city centre, within walking distance of the Victoria Intercontinental Hotel, where we stayed. Tourism there was in its infancy and the city still had a very Soviet feel. The Polish zloty was very weak, and having £100 in my wallet made me a (zloty) millionaire.

During my time in Warsaw, I was expected to write an interim report. The IT manager in USIT, Tony Mosiman, had loaned me his Compaq notebook and I used WordPerfect (an early word processor) and Lotus 123 (a spreadsheet program) for the first time. It was a daunting experience and I struggled to format pages but eventually I saved my work on a floppy disk and arranged for it to be printed.

Being in Warsaw was uneventful until Monday 19 August, when conservative members of the Communist Party of the Soviet Union attempted to depose Mikhail Gorbachev in a coup d'état in Moscow. The events in Russia had a ripple effect, and within a few days, both Estonia and Latvia asserted their right to independence. The coup ended on 21 August, but for a couple of days the atmosphere in Warsaw was tense as the conservative and progressive elements in the new Polish government watched events unfold in Russia.

The Polish economy grew rapidly after the country joined the European Union in May 2004 and today (2024) LOT has a fleet of seventy-five aircraft serving eighty-two destinations. It is a member of the Star Alliance and has developed a strong hub at Warsaw Chopin Airport.

CHAPTER 22

African Flying Boat, 1992

During my time working in southern Africa, I was lucky enough to go to Zimbabwe on several occasions to set up the Lusaka to Harare route for Zambezi Airlines and to evaluate the same route for Proflight a few years later.

Adrian Noskwith

My first trip to Zimbabwe was in September 1992 when a client, Adrian Noskwith, asked me along to help evaluate the commercial viability of a flying boat operation. This was the first but not the last time we'd work together. It was Adrian who involved me in aviation-related projects in the Falkland Islands, Canada and elsewhere. and we developed a friendship that has endured over the years. I'd describe Adrian as a serial entrepreneur with a penchant for out-of-the-box aviation-related projects.

His family background is no less interesting. His parents emigrated to Britain from Germany is the 1930s and set up Charnos, a successful textile business based in Derbyshire. It wasn't until I read a book titled *Enigma* that I learned that Adrian's father, Rolf, had worked in Bletchley Park with Alan Turing and helped break the German navy's Enigma ciphers during World War II. Rolf Noskwith died in 2012 aged ninety-seven and was the last surviving member of Turing's team.

Harare

Adrian and I met up in Harare and stayed in the wonderful, slightly rundown Meikles Hotel, which at the time still had all the jaded elegance of the colonial period. It's since been renovated, but hopefully not too much. In 1992 Harare felt more European than African, with wide streets, modern buildings and parks. There was a landmark steakhouse in Harare where we ate one night. The signature dish was a 2 kg chateaubriand and there was a reward, a free glass of Baileys, if you could finish it.

Flying Boat safari

Adrian was considering an investment in the Catalina Safari Company, having been smitten by the 1990 BBC documentary The Last African Flying Boat. The documentary featured a Catalina flying boat built in Canada in 1944, which was now owned by a French couple, Pierre Jaunet and his wife Antoinette. Pierre's company used the Catalina to operate exclusive air safaris that retraced part of the old Imperial Airways route from Cairo to the Cape.

The capacity of the aircraft was just seventeen passengers and was flown by volunteer Air Zimbabwe pilots for the sheer joy of flying such an iconic aircraft. Pierre was quite a character, fluent in French, English, Italian and Arabic, all very useful if you are flying from Cairo to Victoria Falls.

The itinerary was amazing. It involved taking off from the River Nile in Cairo, flying at 200 ft altitude above the water and finishing at the old Imperial Airways jetty on the Zambezi River near Victoria Falls. Every evening the flying boat would land on the river and moor along the bank adjacent to a tented safari camp or hotel where the guests would overnight.

The price was extraordinary, US $17,000 for the twenty-three-day experience. The passengers were almost exclusively Americans who booked through agents such as Smithsonian Journeys. Pierre said that marketing was not an issue – all the trips were fully booked for the coming year, but he needed an investor. I didn't get to fly on the Catalina but was lucky enough to sit in its lovely cabin and enjoy a drink with Pierre and Antoinette.

Catalina PBY-5A Flying boat built in 1944 and still flying in New Zealand.

Victoria Falls Hotel

Once the business part of the trip was completed, Adrian wanted to see Victoria Falls, so he arranged to charter a four-seat Cessna 172 to take us from Harare to Vic Falls on a day trip. We left mid-morning and the heat thermals created turbulence, which bumped us around for most of the flight. We had lunch in the famous Victoria Falls Hotel, which at the time needed some renovation. However, it was great to be in the venue used for negotiations that eventually lead to a settlement of the war in Southern Rhodesia and the creation of the independent country of Zimbabwe.

Sculptors

Zimbabweans are remarkably talented sculptors, working in springstone, a dark serpentinite stone used in Shona sculpture. There were a few workshops along the road from the city to Harare Airport, including the Shona Sculpture Gallery, where I stopped regularly to admire the work and make a few small purchases. During a visit to Madeira, I visited the Monte Palace Museum, which has an extensive permanent collection of contemporary Zimbabwean sculptures from the period 1966–69.

Unfortunately, Adrian decided not to proceed with his investment, and I never did get to fly on the Catalina flying boat. As part of my research for this book I discovered that while the Catalina no longer operates in Zimbabwe, the company Catalina Safaris is still trading.

Shona Sculpture, Monte Palace Gardens, Madeira.

CHAPTER 23

Ukraine International Airlines, 1992

My long relationship with Ukraine came about in an unexpected way. I was on a family holiday on the Greek island of Paros in late August 1992. One morning I got a fax from my former Ryanair colleague, Derek O'Brien, telling me he was on his way to Ukraine and asking if I would be interested in joining a team setting up a new airline.

Guinness Peat Aviation (GPA) had persuaded the government of newly independent Ukraine to set up a Western-style airline using two leased Boeing 737-400 aircraft. As part of the deal, GPA agreed to send a team of industry experts to manage the set-up of the airline, and on 14 September 1992, I arrived in Kiev to join Derek.

Back story

The Soviet Union had collapsed in 1991 and the constituent countries, including Ukraine, became politically independent. Likewise, the break-up of the leviathan state airline, Aeroflot, spawned so-called 'Babyflots', including Air Ukraine. Aeroflot aircraft based in Ukraine were subsumed into Air Ukraine and continued to operate on many of the old Aeroflot routes.

In making the decision to set up a new airline using Boeing aircraft, the new government in Ukraine recognised that their old fuel-guzzling aircraft had no future when the subsidy on aviation fuel was removed.In another radical move, the Ukrainian government agreed to allow foreign shareholders to own 49 per cent of the airline.

The foreign shareholders – GPA, Swissair, Austrian Airlines and the European Bank for Reconstruction and Development – appointed the vice president and finance director.

We experienced pushback from the management of the state airline, Air Ukraine, who saw no reason to change the status quo.

As a compromise the government agree that Air Ukraine would continue to operate domestic flights and flights to destinations in the former Eastern Bloc, Moscow, Canada and the USA.

Challenges

To differentiate itself from Air Ukraine the new airline was named Air Ukraine International, had its own two-letter IATA booking code (PS), dedicated reservation system and management team.

There was confusion between Air Ukraine and Air Ukraine International, so within a couple of years the new airline became known as Ukraine International Airlines.

Language was a major issue; none of our team spoke Russian and a limited number of government officials spoke English.

Within a short time, GPA recruited a Russian interpreter, Alexander (Sasha) Pasekunov, who helped steer us through the logistical nightmare of doing business in Ukraine. He quickly embraced the Irish sense of humour and helped us find creative solutions to get things done. Yes, it was the same Alexander Pasekunov I had met in Cuba.

There were no direct-dial international telephones in our office, so communications with the outside world were limited to sending telex messages using the SITA airline communications system. As the project cranked up, each member of the team needed to speak daily with external vendors.

To overcome the communications problem, we had a routine whereby Caroline, a long-suffering colleague, in the GPA offices in Shannon would phone us every day and set up a series of conference calls. Caroline would act as a switchboard operator, waiting for us to finish a call and keeping the line open while she set up the next call. Often the line would be open for a couple of hours. Every day brought a new challenge, but eventually the pieces started to slot together.

Training

A select group of ex-Aeroflot pilots who had previously flown Russian-built aircraft were sent on conversion courses and simulator training to enable them to fly the glass-cockpit Boeing 737-400.

The first group of cabin crew were recruited and joined the Aer Lingus safety and service training programme in Dublin, and for the first few months of operation there was an Aer Lingus instructor on most flights.

Uniforms

To break from the Air Ukraine militaristic-looking uniforms with huge hats, we needed a smart, modern uniform. For expediency we settled on a variation of the Ryanair uniform – by coincidence the blue of the Ryanair uniform was almost identical to the blue on the Ukraine national flag. We sourced a tailoring company in Kiev, but they didn't have suitable fabric or buttons. By calling in favours, we managed to buy the cloth and buttons in Ireland.

Air Ukraine operated a weekly flight from New York to Kiev with a refuelling stop in Shannon, so GPA arranged with the handling agent to have the goods loaded onto a flight to Kiev. Customs officers in Kiev Boryspil Airport were 'incentivised', and the uniforms were ready in time for the inaugural flight.

The start-up of Air Ukraine International was viewed sceptically by the wider aviation community, but eventually attitudes changed as airlines such as KLM saw the value of channelling passengers from Kiev to worldwide destinations via their hub at Amsterdam Schiphol Airport. A major milestone was loading the flights into the BABS reservation system, owned at the time by British Airways, enabling travel agents worldwide to make reservations on Air Ukraine International.

Towards the end of October 1992, ground handling and catering contracts were in place, and I began work on the production of technical manuals and marketing collateral. Almost everything from uniform name badges to airport signs had to be imported from Ireland.

First B737-400; the name later changed to Ukraine International Airlines (UIA).

The monkey man

Improvisation was the name of the game. It was my job to design and erect signage at the sales offices in Kiev and Kiev Boryspil Airport. There were no suitable signage contractors in Ukraine, so for a quick, quality job I contracted with Owen Lennon Signs in Dublin.

They needed measurements and photographs of each site, so I borrowed a camera and took photos of the sites; the challenge was to get the film developed. There were no mobile phones or digital cameras and pharmacies didn't offer film developing as they did in Ireland. All was not lost: on Khreshchatyk (the main street in Kiev) there was a man who took souvenir photos of his pet monkey perched on your shoulder.

I hatched a plan to get the 'monkey man' to develop and print my signage photos. The photographer was initially bemused, but money changed hands and I picked up the prints the following week.

Radio licence

In the Soviet era, aircraft in Ukraine were licensed centrally in Moscow. The two aircraft for Air Ukraine International were the first Western aircraft imported into the former USSR, so it was the first time that Ukrainian authorities were faced with the legal oversight of aircraft licensing. Aeroplanes need to have a radio licence issued by the national Civil Aviation Authority (CAA) but in the case of Ukraine there was no template – they'd never done it before. I offered to help, and using a mix of Word and PowerPoint, I created the design for the first radio licence issued in Ukraine.

Inaugural flight

The two Boeing 737-400 aircraft were delivered in early November, flown from Seattle by Boeing pilots who supervised the newly qualified Ukrainian pilots.

The inaugural flight from Kiev to London Gatwick was planned for 25 November 1992. In addition to London, the airline began flights to Amsterdam, Frankfurt, Berlin and Vienna shortly afterwards.

There were only a handful of revenue passengers booked on the inaugural flight to London, so we invited a delegation from the British Embassy, press, foreign airline representatives, travel agents and government dignitaries to boost the numbers.

There was a tremendous sense of occasion on board, and when we arrived in Gatwick the flight was met by senior airport management and the media. I was collared by a journalist and asked to do an interview for Radio 4 to be broadcast the following Saturday morning. I was really surprised by the number of people who said they'd heard me on the radio.

The catering for the return flight to Kiev was arranged by the Aer Lingus catering supplier at Heathrow – it was slightly bizarre to be eating Aer Lingus-branded executive class meals en route back to Kiev.

Solo to Amsterdam

The first flight from Kiev to Amsterdam operated the following week. As I had set up the ground-handling and catering agreements in Amsterdam, it was agreed that I would travel on the first flight.

Unfortunately, there were no bookings. The only passengers were the crew, an Aer Lingus instructor and me. As we taxied towards the gate in Schiphol, I got a glimpse of a large welcoming committee, including young women dressed in traditional Dutch costumes and holding bunches of tulips. When the front door was opened, the ramp agent boarded and greeted me. He then looked behind the bulkhead and got a shock to see there were no passengers. The reception party were very gracious; there were speeches, toasts, and forty minutes later we returned to Kiev. Once again there were no passengers, but we'd enough tulips to open a florist shop.

Hotel Rus – our home in Kyiv.

Hotel Rus

Our home in Kiev was the Hotel Rus, overlooking the football stadium. As the start-up team grew and was augmented by ad-hoc visiting consultants, we had ten rooms on a semi-permanent basis. The room rates were so cheap that we never bothered to check out when we went away on business trips or home to Ireland for the weekend.

The place was basic, and the restaurant menu was still very Soviet – a multi-page menu but most options were 'off'. The result was that we ate a lot of chicken Kiev, boiled potatoes and salad (which was pickled vegetables). However, the 'champagne' was the equivalent of US $3 per bottle and the local beer was cheap. Every Saturday evening there was a dinner dance where couples danced to recorded music. 'The Lady in Red' by Chris de Burgh was a big favourite – the dance floor filled each time it was played.

The ministry supplied a minibus, complete with curtains and a strange smell of gas, to take us to and from the office. There was no café or restaurant scene in Kiev, so lunch was served in a small 'executive' dining room in the Department of Transport building. The menu was limited to fried meat, Ukrainian borsch and varenyky, meat-filled dumplings. The beverage choice was sickly sweet fizzy orange or a highly aromatic local mineral water, thereafter known affectionately as Swamp Water.

I was actively involved in the airline for the first six months of operation, and over the next ten years I did a number of short-term projects. Kiev today is dramatically different to the Kiev of 1992 and at the time of the Russian invasion in February 2022, Ukraine International was operating eleven aircraft.

By 2020 Ukraine International had developed an extensive network.

CHAPTER 24

Romania, 1993

In summer 1993 I worked on an EU-funded marketing project to assist the Ministry of Tourism in Romania to develop a new range of marketing collateral. The ministry's offices were directly opposite the Palace of the Parliament, known locally as Ceausescu's Palace.

President Ceausescu himself was executed on Christmas Day 1989. Even today it remains one of the world's largest government buildings, with a floor area 365,000 square metres.

The project went well, and I designed new branding and a range of marketing collateral such as leaflets, posters, point-of-sale displays, etc.

At the time Bucharest was a very 'basic' city and I felt uncomfortable walking alone around the city at night. I was surprised at the number of Romanian words that I could understand. The language evolved at the beginning of the second century when the Romans conquered the territory of Dacia. The name Romania comes from the Latin word 'Romanus', which means 'citizen of the Roman Empire'.

Transylvania

One weekend a colleague from the Ministry of Tourism offered to show me something of the countryside. We drove north towards Transylvania, commonly associated with vampires, thanks to the character of Dracula created by Dublin-born Bram Stoker.

The scenery was stunning;

Bran Castle, Transylvania.

we drove along the edge of the Carpathian Mountains and vast areas of forestry. Away from Bucharest in more rural areas I was surprised to see horse-drawn ploughs and carts still in daily use, something that had disappeared in Ireland by the 1960s.

Our ultimate destination was Bran Castle about 200 km from Bucharest and 30 km from the regional capital, Brasov. Bram Stoker based his vampire count on a real-life fifteenth-century Romanian nobleman Vlad Tepes (the Impaler), who was infamous for skewering his enemies on stakes. Tepes lived in Bran Castle, a dead ringer for Dracula's mountain lair as described in Stoker's novel. Apparently, Bram Stoker had never even heard of Bran Castle, and Dracula owes nothing to Vlad's atrocities. At the time of my visit, the castle was very dilapidated, but apparently it's since been developed into a Dracula-themed visitor attraction.

On the way back to Bucharest, we stopped off at a restaurant in Brasov for a late lunch. It was memorable for the good local food and wine and for a couple of talented musicians playing 'Flight of the Bumblebee' by Rimsky-Korsakov.

Ceausescu's Palace, was removed and is now a museum.

CHAPTER 25

Dutch Windward Islands, 1994

The Dutch Windward Islands are in the north-eastern part of the Caribbean and comprise the islands of Saba, Saint Eustatius and Saint Martin, known collectively as the SSS islands or the Windward Islands.

The largest of the island group, Saint Martin, is 87 sq. km and is politically divided between France and the Netherlands.

Saba is even smaller at 13 sq. km and located 45 km south-west of Saint Martin and dominated by the dormant Mount Scenery volcano.

Saint Eustatius, also known as Statia, is the most remote of the SSS islands and at 21 sq. km is slightly larger than Saba but still small. It made it into the history books by being the first foreign power to recognise the independence of the United States of America, known as the First Salute, on 16 November 1776.

My project was part of an overall tourism promotion strategy focusing on special-interest tourism. Saint Martin is primarily a transportation hub and a major destination for cruise ships but without a unique tourist product. However, both Saint Eustatius and Saba have marine conservation areas and are popular with divers.

The island of Saba is a special municipality within the Kingdom of the Netherlands.

CHAPTER 26

Aviaprima Sochi, 1994

In 1994 my former Ryanair colleague, Derek O'Brien, was awarded a consultancy contract to provide strategic advice to a private airline, Aviaprima, based in Sochi, on Russia's Black Sea coast.

Derek put together a small team to travel to Sochi to examine various aspects of the airlines operations with a view to giving the owner, Mr Sukarnov, advice on his future strategy. My role in the team was to examine the commercial operation of the airline, including its route network, pricing, distribution and customer service.

Flying to Sochi
In February 1994, Derek and I made our first visit to Sochi. We were booked to fly from Vnukovo Airport in Moscow on a Tu-154 aircraft operated by Vnukovo Airlines, which was founded in 1993 as a spin-off of Aeroflot.

We were invited to the airport VIP lounge overlooking the snow-covered tarmac. As VIPs we were preboarded and brought to the aircraft in a minibus. We sat down in what we thought were our assigned seats only to discover that on Aeroflot aircraft the seat numbers on the back of the seats were not always aligned with the seat numbers overhead. When other passengers boarded there was a great deal of confusion as we were sitting in the wrong seats.

I heard raised angry voices at the front of the cabin – it seemed the flight was overbooked and the cabin crew were trying to offload a few passengers. The arrival of heavyset security men brought the debate to an end, and as we looked out the window, we saw the unfortunate overbookings trudging stoically through the snow back to the terminal.

In-flight hot dogs
The flight to Sochi took almost four hours, and around forty-five minutes into

the flight, the cabin crew started the catering service. I was in the aisle seat behind Derek, and I could see that a cabin crew member was offering him a hot dog from a stainless-steel dish of boiling water perched perilously on the catering trolley. Derek politely refused but the passenger in the window seat indicated that he would like one.

The cabin crew member speared a hotdog, placed it in a folded slice of bread, handed it to Derek, who was expected to pass it to the man in the middle seat, who in turn handed it to the passenger next to the window. When it came to my turn I politely passed on the grub.

What about vodka?
Having left the snow and cold of Moscow, it was lovely to see the blue waters of the Black Sea and to be in a Mediterranean climate. When we disembarked in Sochi, we were met by a car and brought to the VIP lounge in the terminal building where we met the president of the airline, Mr Sukarnov. His English was very limited but through our interpreter, Sasha, he conveyed warm greetings and his pleasure at having us in Sochi. We were ushered into an anteroom, where a table was groaning with a selection of cold meats, salads, etc., Russian style. Although it was only mid-morning, the rest of our day was effectively written off when Mr Sukarnov said in broken English, 'What about vodka?'

Later in the year I was back in Sochi with a couple of other team members. A minibus had been arranged to take us to our hotel, which Derek insisted was a Radisson. We dismissed this as a joke because our previous accommodation in Russia and Ukraine was always in very basic Soviet-era-style hotels. So, it was quite a shock when we turned a corner and arrived at the entrance of the newly opened multi-storey Radisson Hotel. We were like children – cable TV and international telephones – we were in heaven.

Saint Patrick's Day
One of our stays in Sochi coincided with Saint Patrick's Day, and the Scandinavian chef in the Radisson was persuaded to make Irish stew, which we washed down with copious amounts of the local Crown Vodka.

The neck of the bottle was unusual in that there were two magnets on the inside of the neck, which supposedly neutralised any chemicals in the vodka.

I never found any scientific evidence to support the claim, and subsequent hangovers suggest it was just a marketing gimmick.

In the days of the USSR, Sochi was a holiday and spa resort where workers from factories and state enterprises were entitled to two weeks paid holidays; more recently Sochi was host to the Winter Olympics.

The climate was wonderful and it's probably the only place in that part of Europe where there are tea plantations.

Sochi Airlines AviaPrima TU-154 aircraft.

CHAPTER 27

Eritrea, 1994

My contract with Eritrean Airlines came through an Irish aircraft leasing company, which was ultimately being funded by a Kuwaiti investment company that wanted to develop a mobile phone network in Eritrea. The country became an Italian colony in the 1882 and remained so until 1941, when it was placed under British administration until 1950.

It became a province of Ethiopia in 1962 and that led to a war of independence that lasted until 1993 when Eritrea became independent.

I was part of a small team that focused on the core disciplines that would be required for Eritrean Airlines to transition from being solely an airport-handling agent to a fully-fledged regional airline

Getting to Asmara
The flight from London to Addis Ababa was on an Ethiopian Airlines Boeing 757 that made a transit stop in Frankfurt. On arrival in Addis Ababa, I transferred to another Ethiopian Airlines flight to Asmara, the capital of Eritrea, a flight of around an hour and fifteen minutes. This was my first visit to that part of Africa, and during the two-hour layover in Addis Ababa I was blown away by the appearance of other travellers waiting in the transfer lounge.

The women were universally tall and sallow-skinned, and many had a small Coptic Christian cross tattooed on their wrist. Both men and women were dressed in exotic costumes reflecting the culture of the countries in the region – I felt very underdressed.

The Italian influence, in terms of the architecture, food and culture still existed. I really enjoyed my time in Asmara; there were still family-run Italian restaurants serving Italian wines such as Ruffino in straw-covered bottles. On the first trip, I stayed in a hotel on palm-tree-lined Harnet Avenue in the centre of Asmara, and subsequently the consultancy team stayed in a large villa in the suburbs. The people in Eritrean Airlines were very hospitable, as were all the Eritreans we met

Under the stars
One evening the project team were invited to dinner, which we assumed would be served in our hotel or one of the restaurants in Asmara. However, a minibus picked us up and we drove out of town for about forty-five minutes to a remote mountainous area; Asmara is at 2,300 metres altitude. The restaurant was more like someone's house, lit with candles and oil lamps – we were way off the national grid. For the main course we were treated to zigini, a spicy meat stew, considered to be the national dish of Eritrea, served with a type of flatbread.

The highlight of the evening was a coffee ceremony, which took place on an outdoor terrace. It began when the guests were seated on low stools around a small charcoal brazier. Our waiter proceeded to roast coffee beans until they were dark brown, after which he ground the beans and added some ginger. Because there was no light pollution, the sky was full of stars that seemed close enough to touch. It was a special evening.

Eritrean Airlines
Although Eritrean Airlines had been set up by the government in 1991, it had no aircraft. Its only activity was as the ground-handling agent at Asmara International Airport. At the time of my visit, the only direct flights from Asmara were to Addis Ababa and a weekly Lufthansa flight to Frankfurt via Cairo.

Technology workarounds
After thirty years of working in a conflict zone, the local management were very resourceful and had developed creative workarounds. I saw an example of this when I went to the airport to observe passenger check-in and boarding of an Ethiopian Airlines flight to Addis Ababa.

I asked if they used the worldwide SITA telex message system to send post-departure movement messages. I was told yes and invited to step behind the counter to visit the flight dispatch office. An operations officer was sitting at the keyboard of a SITA telex machine composing the so-called movement message to be sent to Ethiopian Airlines informing them of the flight's departure time from Asmara. When the message was typed, I noticed that only a hard copy was printed and asked why. 'This machine isn't connected. We have to bring the printout to the communications office in another building at the end of the apron.'

The operations officer tore off the printout and invited me to follow him. We drove along the apron towards the end of the runway to the communications office, a small, dilapidated brick building. Inside were a couple of wooden desks and broken chairs. I couldn't believe what happened next: the operations officer handed the printout to an older man who proceeded to send the message by morse code – something from a different era.

Project outcome

The management of Eritrean Airlines rejected the findings of our report as too conservative and later opted for a more ambitious plan to lease wide-body aircraft. In April 2003, they started operations between Asmara and Amsterdam, and since then they have operated various-sized older aircraft on several routes; their status is unknown.

Asmara.

Italian Art Deco architecture in Asmara.

CHAPTER 28

Air Atlantic, Canada, 1995

My involvement with Air Atlantic began with a phone call from my client, Adrian Noskwith. He was considering an investment in Air Atlantic, based in Halifax, Nova Scotia, and he wanted someone to examine the airline's commercial operations. Air Atlantic acted as a franchise operator for Canadian Pacific Air Lines (CP), feeding their domestic network in Toronto.

Getting to Halifax involved flying on Aer Lingus to Boston, then taking a connecting flight to Halifax via Saint John in New Brunswick. Halifax was a very pleasant waterfront city with one of the largest and deepest ice-free natural harbours in the world. I stayed at a hotel in the business district close to the Air Atlantic offices. It wasn't all work; one weekend I hired a car and drove along the coast of Nova Scotia to the beautiful historic port of Lunenburg, a UNESCO World Heritage Site.

Newfoundland

During my time with Air Atlantic I was asked to inspect the airline's maintenance facility in St John's, Newfoundland. I was booked on an evening flight from Halifax to St John's, which took approximately an hour and forty-five minutes (plus a thirty-minute time change).

The Air Atlantic people in St John's had booked me into a lovely hotel overlooking the harbour. I was having breakfast the next morning and, even though it was the middle of the summer, a large iceberg floated between the harbour entrance, known as the Heads.

People were friendly; I was constantly being greeted with 'How ya gettin' on?' and hearing the weather described as 'splittin' the rocks' in an accent straight from Kilkenny/Wexford. I shouldn't have been surprised, given that 20 per cent of Newfoundlanders claim Irish heritage.

I was taken to dinner by the head of the maintenance department and a couple of his colleagues to a typical Newfoundland restaurant, where they insisted that I try the local delicacy, cod tongue – I won't be adding it to my favourite food list.

Titanic connection

During my time in Halifax, I became aware of the city's connection with the *Titanic*. Halifax was one of the main ports that received both survivors and victims of the *Titanic* disaster. Many of the victims were buried in Fairview Lawn Cemetery, overlooking the harbour in Halifax, the final resting place for over a hundred victims. Some of the dead were never identified and their headstones simply record 15 April 1912 as the day they died. Roman Catholic and Jewish victims are buried in separate cemeteries, and to this day visitors leave flowers on some of the graves.

Knighthawk Air Express

A separate part of my brief was to report on the operations of a small cargo operator, Knighthawk Air Express, which operated two Dassault Falcon jets on behalf of Airborne Express, a US express parcel service. The Knighthawk Air Express contract was to operate a nightly flight from Ottawa to Montreal and then on to the Airborne Express parcel hub in Wilmington, Ohio.

It was agreed that I should experience the entire Knighthawk operation from Ottawa back to Ottawa. I got myself from Halifax to Ottawa and to the Knighthawk hangar in Ottawa Airport, where I met the two pilots. There were no passenger seats on the aircraft, so I was given permission to sit on the jump seat in the cockpit.

We left Ottawa in the early evening with some packages already on board and flew forty minutes to Montreal's Dorval Airport, where we picked up more packages before taking off and flying south to Wilmington.

The airport there was owned by Airborne Express and active for about six

Titanic victims grave at Fairview Lawn Cemetery, Halifax.

hours every night, when over a hundred aircraft landed between 10 p.m. and midnight from all over the USA and parts of Canada. The aircraft operators are given a five-minute window to land; if they were late there were financial penalties. We landed on time and were marshalled to a parking area already almost full of cargo aeroplanes parked wingtip to wingtip.

The moment the engines were shut down, ground personnel opened the cargo doors and began to unload the parcels. These were then taken by truck to a giant warehouse to be sorted into their final destinations. The workers were predominantly students from the local university and retired people happy to have some part-time work.

We were each allocated a bunk in the crew dormitory and slept in our clothes till 3 a.m., when we went back to the aircraft for the return trip to Montreal and Ottawa. It was an incredible operation with tens of thousands of parcels being unloaded, sorted and reloaded onto different aeroplanes.

Air Atlantic DHC-8-102.

Air Atlantic Bae 146-200.

CHAPTER 29

Columbia, 1995

One of my first bosses in USIT, Adrian Foley, left the company to set up Accident and General Insurance Brokers, the first travel insurance brokerage in Ireland aimed at the travel agency market. Package holiday operators made their own-brand travel insurance almost mandatory, so Adrian saw an opportunity to offer a cheaper policy but also give travel agents a generous commission.

Adrian had a well-rehearsed sales technique, which involved taking an egg timer from his briefcase and saying, 'In the time it takes to boil an egg I'll tell you how your agency can earn 40 per cent commission selling our travel insurance,' at which point he'd turn over the egg timer and start his sales spiel.

Stop the clock!

Adrian loved to tell the story of visiting a travel agency in Dundalk, a town close to the border with Northern Ireland, and asking the receptionist if he could speak to the manager. The receptionist stuck her head around a partition and explained to the manager that he had a visitor. There was some whispered conversation, and she returned to say that the manager was too busy to meet him. Undaunted, Adrian turned over the egg timer and started loudly, 'By the time the egg timer is empty I'll explain how this agency can earn 40 per cent commission selling insurance.' No sooner had he said the words when a disembodied voice with a strong Dundalk accent roared from behind the partition 'Stop the clock!'

Colombia

In 1995 Adrian hired me on a consultancy basis to help with marketing his business, firstly in Ireland and later in Canada under the Bon Voyage brand. The Canadian policy was aimed at the student and academic travel market and was sold exclusively by Travel CUTS, the Canadian national student travel service headed up by my old-time friend, Rod Hurd.

Through a contact in the UK, Adrian was introduced to an insurance company in Colombia that was interested in underwriting a travel insurance policy to be sold through travel agents. Adrian sent me to Bogotá for a couple of weeks to research the market, determine the type of cover that consumers wanted and, most importantly, how the insurance company could collect the premium payments sold by travel agents.

My research revealed that travel insurance being sold in Columbia in 1995 was focused on the medical and twenty-four-hour assistance coverage included with credit card membership.

The travel agents that I interviewed reacted positively to the higher levels of comprehensive cover being proposed for the Bon Voyage policy and the generous commission.

To solve the problem of collecting premiums, I proposed using the existing IATA Bank Settlement Plan that channelled travel agents' sales to IATA, who in turn distributed the revenue to the airlines. My solution was for travel agencies to issue a miscellaneous charges order each time they sold a Bon Voyage policy. Every two weeks IATA would collect payment from the travel agencies by direct debit and pass the premiums to the insurance company.

While Accident and General liked my approach, the challenge of selling to and servicing the Colombian market ultimately resulted in the plan being scrapped.

CHAPTER 30

Armenia, 1996

In early 1996 I was introduced to Armenian Airlines, who needed help in accessing the worldwide travel agency network and getting interline agreements with other airlines.

We agreed terms, and the following week an Armenian Airlines representative in Amsterdam arranged for me to fly to Yerevan. I picked up my ticket at the airline's ticket desk in Schiphol Airport and boarded the Armenian Airlines plane bound for Yerevan. Like all the former Soviet republics, Armenia inherited ex-Aeroflot aircraft, which became the nucleus of a new national airline. My flight was operated by a IL-96 aircraft, designed to carry up to 300 passengers, the only wide body built in the former USSR. It was basically a me-too version of the Airbus A340 but with one innovative twist – passengers could board at ground level and leave their luggage in a left-luggage type storage area before walking up a wooden staircase into the main cabin.

Mount Ararat from my hotel.

The rationale behind this design was that it allowed Aeroflot to operate a wide-body aircraft into remote airports in the USSR, which at the time didn't have airbridges. The design also reduced the instances of lost luggage or delayed baggage because passengers carried their own bags on board.

The flight was punctual and uneventful; the only disconcerting thing was a large domestic TV set perched precariously on a storage cupboard in the middle of the cabin!

Arriving in Yerevan

The flight from Amsterdam to Yerevan took over four hours plus a two-hour time difference. It was after midnight when we landed and I took a taxi to the Bass Boutique Hotel, checked in and headed for bed. I woke up about 6 a.m. It was starting to get light so I got out of bed to pull back the curtains. I was amazed to see Mount Ararat in the distance, it's peak white with snow. Many believe that Mount Ararat is the resting place of Noah's Ark, making the view feel almost spiritual. I later learned the mountain is around 50 km from Yerevan and is in Turkey.

The presence of Mount Ararat just across the border was a daily reminder of the historic animosity that exits between Armenia and Turkey.

Visiting Etchmiadzin

My project stretched over several months, and during one of my visits I learned more about the unique place that Armenia holds in history. In AD 301 the Kingdom of Armenia was the first state to adopt Christianity as its official religion and to this day the Armenian Apostolic Church is one of the custodians of the Church of the Holy Sepulchre in Jerusalem. One weekend I was taken to the city of Etchmiadzin, where the cathedral was built in AD 303, making it the oldest cathedral in the world.

Boney M.

My contact in the airline was Simon Avagyan, the commercial director, who went out of his way to help me both professionally and personally. I had two memorable outings during my time in Yerevan. Firstly, Simon brought me to a Boney M. concert in the arena of a local university. By 1996 Boney M. were well past their prime but they still seemed to be popular in Armenia. The venue was jammed with university students who knew the words of every song, even though most of them probably weren't born when the songs were first hits.

World Cup match

The other outing was to a World Cup qualifier between Armenia and Germany on 9 October 1996 in the Hrazdan Stadium. Simon wanted to go home to change before the game, so we left the office early and drove to his place. He lived in a so-called Khrushchyovka apartment, which were championed by premier Nikita Khrushchev in the 1960s, when millions were built throughout the Soviet Union. It transpired that Simon still lived with his family, and his mother greeted me like royalty; tea was made and a box of chocolates was ceremoniously produced from a glass cabinet. Shortly afterwards his father arrived home and I was surprised that he was in an Armenian Airlines pilot's uniform with captain's stripes. There aren't many Aer Lingus or Ryanair captains who live so modestly.

The game was sold out and I was surrounded by 40,000 animated but good-humoured Armenian fans. Unfortunately, it ended 5–1 to Germany but I did get to see the great Jürgen Klinsmann score.

Armenian Airlines was unable to compete effectively with two private airlines that started in the late 1990s and eventually it ceased operations in 2003.

Yerevan with snow covered Mt.Ararat in the distance.

CHAPTER 31

Falklands Airlines, 1997

The call from Adrian Noskwith came early one wet January morning in 1997. 'Are you busy?' he asked, before telling me he was in Punta Arenas in southern Chile negotiating with a local airline, DAP, to start scheduled flights to the Falkland Islands. He asked me to join him there as soon as possible and said that he would arrange tickets for later that day.

Punta Arenas

I flew from London to Santiago that very afternoon, and when I arrived I was met by a representative of DAP Airlines, whisked through immigration and driven to a DAP aircraft waiting to depart for Punta Arenas. The flight was operated by a Boeing 727, and I was the only passenger in first class.

I was invited to the cockpit, where I sat in the jump seat for most of the flight. The views were staggering; our routing took us almost due south along the spine of the Andes, with the ocean to the right. When we landed in Punta Arenas it was still daylight and the roadsides were covered with summer lupins.

Stanley, Falkland Islands.

Arriving in the Falklands

I met Adrian in the hotel, and the next day, 15 January 1997, we flew to the Falklands from Punta Arenas on a chartered King Air turboprop aircraft; not for the faint-hearted. Although the Falklands War had ended in 1982, the immigration procedures and security at Mount Pleasant Airport were robust. We stayed in the iconic Malvina House Hotel, whose claim to fame was that Margaret Thatcher stayed there on her visit to the Falklands in 1983.

One of a fleet of five Britten-Norman BN-2 Islander aircraft.

Air Taxi service

As part of our consultation process, I met with the general manager of the Falkland Islands Government Aviation Service (FIGAS), which was more of an air taxi service than a scheduled airline. Its role was to provide a lifeline to the many sheep-farming families living on the outlying islands and tiny communities, locally known as 'Camp'. One of the walls in the FIGAS office was dominated by a large map of the Falkland Islands with wool attached to drawing pins. This turned out to the be tomorrow's schedule for each of their fleet of seven-seater Britten-Norman Islander aircraft – there was a different colour wool for each aircraft. Seeing that I was puzzled, one of the ops officers explained how it worked.

Anyone wishing to travel had to phone or radio FIGAS with their travel requirements by 10 a.m. the day before they intended to travel; the FIGAS operations department then planned the next day's timetable. The final schedule was published every afternoon and broadcast on the local radio station, where confirmed passengers were given their departure times. When I asked how fares were calculated I was told, 'That's easy; we charge one pound per mile.'

Falkland Island Airways

Adrian had arranged several meetings with potential stakeholders of the proposed new airline. Because the Falkland Islands are an internally self-governing overseas territory of the United Kingdom, we also met with the governor, as well as tourism and business interests on the islands. While there was general support for an air route to the South American mainland, there were concerns both about a flight from Argentina and the possible impact on the weekly RAF flight from the UK, which provided seats for civilians.

I was commissioned to explore the feasibility of establishing a new airline based in the Falkland Islands that would initially operate a twice-weekly connection between Stanley and São Paulo (via Montevideo). The report would also explore the possibility of the new carrier also operating the Stanley–Punta Arenas route, in cooperation with the existing operator, Aerovías DAP.

Critical to the success of the proposed new airline was negotiating a franchise or code share agreement with British Airways. In practical terms this would mean the new airline flying in BA colours, with a BA flight number, etc. giving the airline immediate brand recognition and the benefits of BA's extensive worldwide sales network. If the proposed new airline was a BA franchise it would be possible to offer connecting passengers a seamless service.

São Paulo and Montevideo

While Adrian lobbied for support at BA corporate level, I was tasked with discussing the idea with the British Airways management in Brazil and Uruguay. The BA manager in São Paulo was supportive of the idea because the extension of the London–São Paulo flight to Montevideo would open a new route. I then flew to Montevideo to meet with the British Airways general sales agent in Uruguay. There were no direct flights from São Paulo, so I routed via Buenos Aires and took a short connecting flight across the River Plate estuary to Montevideo. On the final descent into Montevideo Airport, I caught a glimpse of the World War II German battleship *Graf Spee*, which was scuttled during the 1939 Battle of the River Plate and now rested in 25 ft of water just off the coast.

Montevideo had a 1950s feel, with elegant squares and European-style architecture. I had an excellent dinner of beef cooked on a traditional *parrilla* grill and served by old-school waiters in tuxedos.

Return to the Falklands

I was scheduled to return to the Falklands a couple of months later and was booked on the weekly RAF flight from Brize Norton air force base outside Oxford. Check-in was utilitarian, and judging by the crew-cut hairstyle of most of the passengers, I was one of the few civilians on the flight. The flight was subject to a creeping delay and was eventually cancelled due to adverse weather conditions on Ascension Island, where the plane was due to refuel; I never did experience Royal Air Force in-flight service.

I made my way from Oxford to Heathrow, and the next day I took a scheduled flight to Santiago and onwards to Punta Arenas and from there to the Falklands. The feasibility report was well received but a combination of local and international politics effectively scuppered the plan; perhaps it was too ambitious, or the right idea at the wrong time.

Irish salmon

I travelled home via Punta Arenas, Puerto Montt, Santiago, Miami and New York. On the first leg the flight stopped at the Chilean port city of Puerto Montt. The final approach was over the sea, and from the air I noticed that there were dozens of salmon cages strung across the bay.

It was only years later that my pal Tony Fox told me that most of the salmon there had started their lives as tiny fry born in his fish farm in Donegal and sent by air freight from Belfast to Amsterdam and on to Chile.

ISLANDER BRAVO OSCAR	2nd FLIGHT		CHECK-IN TIME: 1010 TBC
STANLEY, ALBEMARLE, WEDDELL AND STANLEY			
STANLEY	Departures:	Mr J Wilson, Ms R Laidlaw & Mrs N Smith	
ALBEMARLE	Arrivals: Departures:	Mr J Wilson & Ms R Laidlaw Miss H May	
WEDDELL ISLAND	Arrivals: Departures:	Mrs N Smith Mr S Clifton, Ms J Turner, Master T Clifton & Master P Clifton	

Example of Air Taxi pick-ups and drop-offs.

CHAPTER 32

Tuvalu, 1997

In early 1997 I was approached by CHL Consulting and asked if I would be interested in a medium-term assignment as tourism marketing advisor for Tuvalu. I gave my usual qualified yes and then went looking for Tuvalu on my *National Geographic Atlas*. Tuvalu was previously part of the Gilbert and Ellice Islands and in October 1978 they got independence from the UK. Kiribati, formerly the Gilbert Islands, became independent in July 1979.

Like elsewhere, the UK had created a political unit without much regard to cultural factors; in this case the indigenous people in the Gilbert Islands were Micronesians, whereas the people in Tuvalu were Polynesians. It's therefore not surprising that they opted to become two independent nations; the Gilbert Islands became Kiribati, and the Ellice Islands became Tuvalu.

The overall project was managed by the Tourism Council of the South Pacific (TCSP) from their offices in Suva, the capital of Fiji. As I started to do my travel planning, the size and remoteness of the region became clearer – just to get to Nadi, the international airport in Fiji, was an eleven-hour flight from Dublin to Los Angeles, another ten hours to Nadi and a final thirty-minute puddle-jumper flight from Nadi to Suva.

Even though Nadi and Suva are only 115 km apart, Nadi was usually warm and dry, Suva was the opposite – the British clearly felt more at home in rainy Suva. I spent a few days in the TCSP offices meeting the team, getting a full briefing, and preparing for my assignment on Tuvalu.

If I thought that Fiji was remote, Tuvalu was even more remote – the capital, Funafuti, was a further 1,000 km north of Fiji. Tuvalu itself had a total population of just 11,000 people and comprised nine islands spread over a sea area the size of France – now that's remote.

Flying to Funafuti
The air service to Tuvalu was very limited; the route from Suva to Funafuti

operated three times weekly with a fifty-seat aircraft, which continued to Tawara in Kiribati and Majuro in the Marshall Islands. The flight to Funafuti took two and a half hours, with nothing to see below except the vast expanse of the Pacific Ocean.

I got my first glimpse of Funafuti as we did a complete circuit of the atoll before landing on the runway built by the American forces in 1942. Because the airport doesn't have a security fence, a klaxon is sounded, and arriving flights do a low-level fly-past to clear people, dogs and pigs off the runway.

Only five people disembarked – most of the passengers were bound for Tawara or Majuro and they stayed on board during the short transit stop.

I picked up my bags and watched as the plane taxied and took off, not to be seen again for another couple of days. My transfer to the hotel was easy – it was a two-minute walk from the terminal building. The twenty-room Vaiaku Lagi Hotel was built in 1993 with financial assistance from the government of Taiwan and was my home for the next month or so.

Life on Tuvalu
Most people lived in two-storey traditional wooden houses with thatched or galvanised-iron roofs – the living space was an open-plan area upstairs, with the ground floor being used for storage.

At the time of my visit Tuvalu, tourism consisted of about 1,000 visitors a year, a sizeable percentage being people like me on government-related business, plus a small number of intrepid travellers. Funafuti and the other atoll islands are all low-lying, with no point in Tuvalu being higher than 4.5 metres above sea level. The soil is not generally suitable for farming, with rising sea levels, flooding, and drought having an adverse impact on the limited cultivation of food crops, particularly on staples such as pulaka and taro. Fresh water was harvested solely from rainwater and stored in concrete tanks in front of houses.

My first couple of weeks involved working with my Tourism Department counterpart to gain product knowledge and to listen to the views of the stakeholders. Understandably, people were concerned about the impact of tourism on their way of life. The dilemma being that while tourism can create much-needed employment, too many visitors impact on the local culture and resources.

Product development

One of my first recommendations was to develop special-interest activities aimed at incoming visitors, expatriates and locals.

I was explaining this strategy to my government counterpart, and he asked for an example of the activities that could be developed. I said, 'Maybe one of the boat owners could offer fishing trips at weekends when expats like me are not working.' About a week later I was having a beer in the hotel bar and one of the local fishermen approached me and introduced himself as the skipper of a fishing boat. 'I hear you'd like to go fishing. We're going out tomorrow night if you're interested.' We agreed terms and he told me not to worry about tackle or bait and to be outside the hotel at ten o'clock.

Gone fishing

The skipper picked me up in a battered jeep and we drove a short distance to the dock. A group of other fishermen were loading large cooler boxes and supplies onto a 30 ft half-deck fishing boat with a small wheelhouse. We cast off and within about ten minutes we stopped in the middle of the lagoon and the locals started fishing.

When I asked about joining in, the skipper explained that he'd stopped to catch small bait fish – the real fishing would be outside the lagoon. The electrics on the boat didn't seem to be working so we had to rely on moonlight and few oil lamps.

With the bait fish caught, we sailed through a narrow gap in the reef out into the ocean, and in about half an hour the engine was cut and the fishing began. I was naively expecting a 'big-game' fishing experience but what I got instead was a large hook attached to heavy duty line weighed down with bits of old iron. The skipper baited my hook with half a mackerel and gestured to me to find myself some space and start fishing. By the time I'd dropped my line overboard my fishing companions were hauling fish over the side and filling up the cooler boxes. Within minutes of starting, I felt a bite and I started to pull the catch to the surface – there was no real technique – just brute force to pull the fish into the boat. I was disappointed when my bait fish came into view with only his head on the hook. The skipper explained that a barracuda had probably snatched the rest of the body.

In the next few hours, we landed plenty of big fish, including barracuda,

Busy day at Funafuti Airport.

tuna, mahi-mahi and wahoo. By about 4 a.m. I was getting tired, so I found myself a space on the deck, lay on my back and looked up at the stars. The night air was balmy, and with the gentle rocking of the boat I drifted off to sleep for about an hour and only woke when the engine started up for the return trip.

When we docked, it was getting bright and the cooler boxes were offloaded onto the quay. I was invited to choose a fish; it was explained that the hotel would put it in the refrigerator and cook it for that night's dinner. I choose a mahi-mahi, which was then cleaned and filleted.

The next time I met the skipper, I enthused about my experience and said it would be an excellent tourist activity.

I asked, 'So when will you be going out fishing again?'

The skipper seemed surprised by my question and replied, 'When we need more fish.'

It was a textbook example of a subsistence economy – great for the planet but not easy to market as a tourism product.

Making the salt run

I ate most of my meals in the hotel and I was on first-name terms with the restaurant staff. Because of the limited supply of fresh vegetables, the menu was rather bland and uninspiring. The food needed a sprinkling of salt, but the high humidity meant that none of the salt cellars worked. During dinner you'd hear the bashing of salt cellars on the table as frustrated diners tried to get the salt out.

Eventually I had a quiet word with the restaurant manager and politely explained that adding a few grains of rice would absorb dampness and allow the salt to flow. She promised to give it a try and that evening when I arrived for dinner the expat diners all stood up, picked up their salt cellars and shook salt onto their tables – I then got a round of applause! Some smart ass said loudly that while I might not solve Tuvalu's tourism problems, I'd be forever remembered as the consultant who got the salt to flow in Tuvalu, albeit at huge cost to the EU taxpayer.

About ten years later I read that a couple of representatives from the Irish Department of Foreign Affairs visited Tuvalu to lobby the government to support Ireland's bid for one of the rotating seats on the UN Security Council in 2001. I sometimes wonder if they were told that a fella from Ireland had been there a few years previously and made the salt flow. Perhaps my efforts in some small way had contributed to Ireland being elected to a security council.

New friendships

My daily routine was to get up early, swim in the lagoon before breakfast and then walk the short distance to my office in the government building. The working day was 8 a.m. to 4 p.m., and after work I'd have another swim.

One day I was returning from my afternoon swim and was surprised to see the next-door room open and a couple of guys sitting outside on the balcony with a large bottle of coke, a bucket of ice and a bottle of Bundaberg Rum, better known as Bundy. We exchanged greetings and then I was invited to join them for a sundowner, and this became a daily ritual for the remainder of their time on Tuvalu.

Both guys were taking part in a New Zealand government programme to assist the smaller Pacific islands with law enforcement issues – Garry was an immigration officer based in Christchurch and Colin a police officer with the drug squad in Auckland. Their mission in Tuvalu was to train the local constabulary on how to stem the flow of drugs onto the island by targeting young Tuvaluan men returning home having worked on merchant ships. Remittances from Tuvaluans living in Australia and New Zealand, and remittances from merchant seamen were important sources of income for Tuvaluans.

On the first day of training, the full law enforcement complement of ten constables and one sergeant showed up, but by the end of the week the attendance had dropped to the sergeant and two constables.

During one of our chats, I explained that Jackie had a cousin married to a retired policeman from Christchurch named Bill Tarre, who had been a dog handler. Garry immediately said, 'I know the bloke. He was a real tough character.' Small world indeed.

I hooked up with both Garry and Colin on future trips to NZ, and Colin and his wife Raelene stayed with us when they came to Dublin for an Ireland v All Blacks game. Colin still talks about standing outside Slattery's on Shelbourne Road drinking pints of Guinness.

Happy ending

When my project ended, I wrote a report with my findings and recommendations that were later included in a tourism development master. I had nagging doubts that sustainable tourism alone would ever be a major economic gamechanger. But then, through a series of serendipitous events Tuvalu hit the jackpot when the International Telecommunication Union assigned it the national web designator .tv (think www.u.tv). It's estimated that Tuvalu earns over $10 million a year in royalties, thanks to increased demand for use of .tv

Tuvalu has a regular income without having to deal with the downside of tourism. A rare win-win in tourism development.

CHAPTER 33

Coast Starlight, California, 1997

Taking the train

In 1997 I was doing a project that included meetings in both San Francisco and Los Angeles. Rather than drive or fly, I opted to take the Amtrak Coast Starlight Train, which operates daily from Seattle to Los Angeles via Portland and San Francisco. As trains no longer stop in downtown San Francisco, my journey started at the San Francisco Ferry terminal where I took a shuttle bus to nearby Oakland.

When I travelled in 1997, train travel was enjoying somewhat of a revival in the United States after decades of neglect. The Amtrak terminal at the San Francisco Ferry terminal was modern, clean and staffed by friendly folk who issued my ticket and took care of my baggage, airline style. The fare at $62 single, and without the irritating airport taxes, worked out at about $5 an hour.

The Thruway Amtrak bus to Oakland station departed on schedule at 8.45 a.m. and within minutes we were speeding across the Bay Bridge, less famous than its neighbour the Golden Gate Bridge, but no less awesome.

Train 11, the Coast Starlight, pulled into Oakland station at 9.25 a.m. and ten minutes later we were ready to depart. I was safely ensconced in seat 21 on the upper deck in a second-class coach seat. Ahead was the sightseeing car – a glass-sided carriage with seats facing to the sides, and the sleeper car. Most of the seats were already occupied by passengers who had joined the train somewhere along its 700-mile journey that started in Seattle, Washington State, the night before. There were few empty seats, but I was lucky enough to have two seats to myself for most of the eleven-hour trip.

For the first couple of hours the Coast Starlight made painfully slow progress through San Jose, Salinas, and several anonymous small towns. It's not fair to judge a country by the view from a passing train but the vista from the sightseeing car was depressing – rubbish strewn along the tracks, countless rusting cars and trucks, and housing normally associated with South African townships. The legacy of the 'disposable society' was everywhere and it was not a pretty sight.

A call over the public address system broke the monotonous rhythm of wheel on track: 'The snack lounge is now open for hot coffee, cold beers and Bloody Marys. Come on down!' What better than an iconic American drink, the Bloody Mary, to complement my very own Great Railway Journey? In the snack lounge I was greeted by a cheerful Chinese-American woman who mixed me an excellent Bloody Mary, complete with Tabasco, seasoning, and Worcestershire sauce. I retired to the comfort of the sightseeing lounge to sip on my drink and watch the world go by.

The rail track wended its way down a narrow coastal plain between a low mountain range and the coast. There were occasional green plains where vegetables are cultivated with the aid of vast irrigation schemes, but otherwise the land looked arid and dusty. Small herds of cattle relied on food and water troughs to survive, but even then, I saw more than one dead animal that had succumbed to the drought.

Just south of San Luis Obispo, about seven hours into the journey, I got my first view of the shimmering Pacific Ocean to the right of the train, beyond some enormous sand dunes. At one point on the left side there were large

Union Station, Los Angeles.

parking lots full of RV vehicles, but soon after the cultivation began again, this time there were fields of peas as far as the eye could see.

There is something about the sound of an American train whistle that evokes long-gone days when the railways criss-crossed the country carrying freight and the dreams of immigrants heading west in search of new beginnings. The trains are no longer steam-driven, but that almost ghostly whistle sound is faithfully reproduced by the modern diesel locomotives.

The most interesting scenery was in the last few hours before arriving in Los Angeles. For over thirty minutes the train passed slowly through pristine countryside, preserved not by Friends of the Earth but a more unlikely benefactor – the US military. The Vandenberg Air Force Base became famous, or rather infamous, as the home for the US Minuteman missile programme: even today the giant silos stand as a permanent reminder of the Cold War. The Space Shuttle had its origins there, and a building, decked with an enormous stars and stripes, that housed launch vehicles still stands proud, even though the programme itself has long been abandoned.

Despite what seemed to be a slow pace and hold-ups along the way, the Coast Starlight arrived in Los Angeles at 9.15 p.m. just ten minutes behind schedule. Union Station is just one of the many iconic old train terminals that are being restored to their former glory.

The thirty-minute wait for checked baggage was the only real irritant on what was otherwise a long but pleasant travelling experience. Long live the train.

Viewing Lounge on the Coast Starlight Train.

CHAPTER 34

Kaliningrad, 1998

Kaliningrad, formerly known as Königsberg, became Kaliningrad when it was occupied by the USSR during World War II. It's now an oblast of modern-day Russia, even though it's an enclave surrounded by Lithuania and separated from Mother Russia. Its strategic value is as an ice-free port on the Baltic Sea. The only land link with Russia is the rail corridor that runs from Kybartai through Lithuania to Kena, on the border with Belarus.

I went there as part of a small EU-funded team asked to prepare an outline feasibility plan for a new airline to eclipse Kaliningrad Avia, the ex-Aeroflot entity based at Kaliningrad Airport.

At the time the only international route to the West was a daily flight between Copenhagen and Kaliningrad, operated by SAS using a fifty-seat Saab aircraft.

Kaliningrad suffered heavy damage from British bombing raids in 1944 – the historic city centre, the cathedral, castle, etc. were all destroyed, but some were subsequently rebuilt.

At the time of my visit in 1998, there was very little tourism and only a handful of hotels and restaurants. It was historically interesting but not on my list of places I'd choose to revisit.

Our recommendations were to create a new airline named Kaliningrad Express that would operate independently from the Kaliningrad Airways with separate management, Boeing aircraft and customer-focused service.

We also recommended the establishment of a free trade zone similar in concept to the Shannon Free Trade Zone pioneered by the Irish government in 1959. Feedback from cargo flight operators was that importing goods via Sheremetyevo International Airport in Moscow was problematic because of corruption and bureaucracy. Having Kaliningrad Airport designated as a free trade zone would have enabled FedEx, DHL, etc. to create a hub where goods could clear Russian customs before being transhipped to other parts of Russia.

There was overall acceptance of our recommendations, but on the day we were leaving Kaliningrad to return to Dublin, the Russian government devalued the rouble. The resulting Russian financial crisis created economic turmoil, and the plans to remodel Kaliningrad aviation were shelved.

Kaliningrad Avia went into receivership in 2001 and a new airline, KD Avia, started operations in 2004 and grew to a fleet of nineteen aircraft until it too ceased operations in 2009.

CHAPTER 35

South Pacific Odyssey, 1998

My 1997 assignment in Tuvalu was such an amazing experience that when I was given the opportunity to produce a study on air access and its impact on tourism development in the South Pacific, I jumped at it.

I was based in the Tourism Council of the South Pacific offices in Suva, the capital of Fiji. I lived in a small hotel within walking distance of the office, and at weekends I would watch rugby at the local club. There weren't enough jerseys for the substitutes, so when a player was substituted the departing player would strip off and the sub would wear his jersey.

My project involved interviewing a broad spectrum of South Pacific tourism stakeholders such as airlines, airport operators, destination management companies, government agencies, overseas tour operators, etc. Because of the vastness of the region, it was impossible for me to personally visit every island state, so many of the interviews were done by phone; this was the pre-Zoom era.

The communication logistics were complicated by the international date line, which meant the occasional middle-of-the-night meeting. After my trip, Samoa opted to shift to the west side of the International Date Line so that they were in sync with Australia and New Zealand, their main trading partners.

Niue

As part of the consultive process, it was agreed that I would visit Niue, located west of Fiji and south of Samoa. It's one of the smallest countries in the world but with the largest raised coral atolls. Niue was a self-governing state in free association with New Zealand, and Niueans were considered New Zealand citizens. At the time of Niue's 2017 census, the resident population was 1,590; approximately 90 per cent of Niue's diaspora lived in New Zealand. Niue's 'capital', Alofi, is little more than a large village.

During my visit I met with tourism representatives, government officials, accommodation operators and other interested parties.

My trip coincided with a local festival, and I was invited to a celebratory dinner. My local counterpart drove me from my hotel to the venue, a community hall on the other side of the island. En route we drove past a coastal forest, home to giant coconut crabs that weigh up to 4 kg. He explained to me that this is where locals came at night to hunt the crabs and, right on cue, we saw some of the crabs on the roadway ahead and swerved to avoid them.

The dinner was great fun. The locals were very curious as to who I was and what I was doing there. And, of course, the main dish was curried coconut crab, which was delicious. When I was on Niue, I was introduced to a local artist, Mark Cross, whose work I found fascinating and I still occasionally fantasise about buying one of his works.

Given the size of the island, there is very little more that can be done to grow tourism, but it still attracts intrepid travellers.

Kingdom of Tonga

My visit to Tonga was a couple of weeks after His Majesty Tāufaʻāhau Tupou IV celebrated his eightieth birthday. King Tāufaʻāhau Tupou IV had the dubious honour of being the heaviest monarch in the world. Whenever he made overseas state visits, the hosts had to build special reinforced ceremonial chairs to support his 200 kg; although later he did go on a diet for charity. Apparently, the king thought these chairs were gifts and arranged for them to be shipped home.

On the way into town from the airport, I passed what looked like a rugby pitch ,where workers were dismantling a marquee and taking down flags and bunting. The taxi driver explained that this was where the king had recently hosted a communal eightieth birthday feast where everyone was welcome. Because of the strict social hierarchy in Tonga, I'm not sure how much roast pork was left for the average citizen.

In common with most South Pacific countries, whole pigs were cooked for seven to eight hours in a large underground pit or spit roasted over hot coals.

I met with Jim Bradfield, the GM of Royal Tongan Airlines, who explained the difficulty of operating a scheduled airline in small markets.

Unfortunately, but not unusually, there was political interference in the management of the airline, and it eventually went bankrupt in 2004 with debts of US $8 million, which was spectacular for such a small airline in such a small country.

Royal Nukuʻalofa Club

Because I'd crossed the international date line, I enjoyed two successive Friday night drinks. Jim suggested we go for a drink in his club, the grandly named Royal Nukuʻalofa Club, founded in 1914 and described then as a 'private club where gentlemen came to relax and have a drink'.

Although it was just after 6 p.m., there were no seats available in the lounge, so we sat at the bar and ordered a couple of beers. The place had the jaded charm of an English gentleman's club.

We were chatting away, and I casually looked around and said, 'Not many women in here tonight.' The reaction was immediate – the bar went totally quiet and there was a lot of muttering. Eventually a disembodied voice from the corner said, 'I say, chaps, didn't we have a member named Roberts? His bloody wife kept phoning, so we had to drum the bugger out.' There was some more muttering and then the normal conversation resumed.

CHAPTER 36

South Africa, 1998

Early in 1998 I was contacted by a friend from my student travel days, Laurine Platsky, who was working for the Western Cape Government in South Africa. Part of her brief was to help the provincial government find a medium-term solution to overcrowding at Cape Town International Airport. I was asked to follow up on a proposal to allow civilian flights to use the South African Air Force training base in Langebaanweg on the coast, about an hour's drive north of Cape Town.

My brief was to investigate the operational and commercial implications of operating direct flights from Langebaanweg to Johannesburg. I based myself in Cape Town and used a hire car to travel to Langebaanweg, where I began my market research with meeting the travel agency community in the area. The travel agents seemed to think that a direct flight to Johannesburg would be popular, and they provided me with details of the number of tickets they sold from Cape Town to Johannesburg and beyond. Based on that data I was able to extrapolate the possible demand for a direct feeder service from Langebaanweg to Johannesburg.

I contacted Roger Foster, the CEO of Airlink, which at the time had a franchise agreement with South African Airways (SAA) to provide feeder flights from domestic airports to SAA's hub in Johannesburg. His initial response was positive, but understandably he wanted more data before the new route could be considered.

The most important step was to discuss the idea with the South African Air Force base commander at Langebaanweg, without whose support the plan would go nowhere.

Contacts in the provincial government arranged for me to visit the base the following week and to introduce the concept to the commander.

When I got to the main gate of the base, my credentials were checked and I was then escorted to the base commander's office. I was warmly received, shown a map of the base indicating the area that had been identified as a possible site for a small domestic terminal. The commander then suggested that it would be an idea for me to see the actual site. As we drove in his jeep along the taxiway towards the end of the runway and the designated area, we discussed how the arrangement might work in practice.

Our chat was suddenly interrupted by what sounded like an urgent call on the radio and excitable chatter in Afrikaans. The commander apologised and said that he'd need to return immediately to his office to pick up a weapon. I thought that there had been a coup, terrorist attack or something equally dramatic, but on the way back to the office he explained, 'Sorry we'll have to cut this short. I've got to deal with some bloody buck on the runway.'

I presented my report, but nothing ever came of the project, and in early 2000 the government began a large project to redevelop Cape Town International Airport, which opened in 2003.

DUTCH REFORMED CHURCH
FRANSCHOEK, SOUTH AFRICA
24.01.2016

CHAPTER 37

Pakistan, 1998

My reason for going to Pakistan was to join a team contracted to do a strategic review and turnaround plan for Pakistan International Airlines (PIA). The project was being managed jointly by British Airways' consultancy arm, Speedwing, and Sabre, at that time part of American Airlines.

I was part of the Speedwing team investigating the causes and extent of fraud occurring in several Pakistan International Airlines offices in Europe and the US. This involved me visiting the PIA offices in London, Paris, New York and Houston, as well as spending a couple of days in the PIA head office in Karachi.

One of the bonuses of working for a British Airways subsidiary was that all my travel was in business class, something I was not used to.

Most of the fraud was being committed by travel agents, who were at the time using paper tickets. The most common types of fraud was so-called 'cardboarding', which involved charging a customer for a booking made in an unrestricted booking class but paying the airline for a cheaper ticket.

This was done by placing a piece of cardboard between the passenger coupon and the issuing office coupon of the ticket. The agent would write the higher fare booking class on the coupon given to the passenger but a much lower fare was written on the portion of the ticket submitted on the monthly sales report. Another scam was to book and report a child fare while entering an adult name on the portion of the ticket given to the passenger.

At the time, travel within Pakistan was a security risk, so the British Airways security team suggested that my colleague and I use a different route every time we travelled from our hotel to the airport. They also advised us to dress down by taking off our jackets and ties and to travel in an ordinary taxi rather than a hotel limo.

On the other hand, the Americans on the Sabre team were advised to stay in a hotel closer to the airport and to travel with an armed escort. My colleague and I would arrive at the airport in a beaten-up old taxi, whereas the Sabre people arrived in a small convoy with Kalashnikov-toting guards in open-top jeeps.

Having completed our field reports, we were invited to attend a special PIA commercial management meeting held in the mountain resort of Murree about 30 km north-east of Islamabad. Murree is at 2,200 metres altitude and was built by the British Raj to escape the scorching summer heat in the Punjab plains.

The journey by road to Murree was seriously scary but after a couple of hours I arrived safely. The hotel was built in a scenic location from where I was able to look out and see the splendour of the Himalayan mountain range, including K2, the second-highest mountain in the world, shining white in contrast to the blue sky.

The conference itself was uneventful; the recurring theme was a sentimental journey back to the good old days of Pakistan International Airlines. The status of PIA within Pakistani society was still such that the prime minister, Nawaz Sharif , was guest of honour at dinner one evening.

Like at many state airlines there was constant interference by government in the management and direction of the airline, which resulted in overstaffing, poor corporate governance and little regard for customer service.

I was told that when Benazir Bhutto was elected president, the following Monday there were thousands of people at the main entrance of the PIA offices with letters stating that they were to be given a job in the airline.

The final report was well received but it seemed that the senior management were more concerned with maintaining the status quo than tackling the big-picture changes and sacrifices that would be needed to make PIA a viable com-mercial airline.

On my last trip to Pakistan, I purchased a lovely silk rug that still graces the floor in front of the fireplace in our lounge.

Murree was a hill station used by the Raj to escape the summer heat.

CHAPTER 38

Oman, 2003/4

I was sitting in the Shelbourne Hotel in Dublin having lunch with two American friends when my mobile rang. It was the first week of January in 2003 and I was on the lookout for work, so I stepped outside to take the call.

I didn't recognise the number, but the caller introduced herself as Siobhán McGinty from a consultancy firm called International Development Ireland (IDI), which specialised in tourism and international economic development projects. She explained that IDI were looking for a tourism marketing expert on a one-year contract in Oman, starting as soon as possible.

I wouldn't ordinarily have been interested in a long-term assignment, but work was slow, and I was tempted by working in a part of the world where I had never been before. I went home and discussed it with Jackie, and we talked about the implications of me spending so much time away from home.

Our friends Charles and Sheenagh Chapman had spent almost five years in Oman and really enjoyed the experience, so I telephoned Charles asking for his advice. He invited us to dinner the next night and related how much they had enjoyed living in Oman and encouraged us to go for it.

In the spring of 2003, the Americans were leading a campaign against Saddam Hussein's regime in Iraq and friends expressed concern about me going to work in the Middle East. However, I felt confident that I would be in minimal danger given that Muscat was further away from Baghdad than Athens.

I had a formal interview with IDI, during which I learned that the previous marketing expert had left, and IDI were under pressure to replace her as quickly as possible. They forwarded my CV to the ministry responsible for tourism development, who approved my appointment. Jackie spoke to her boss, who was supportive of her taking unpaid leave of absence for six months, which meant that my time alone there wouldn't be as long.

Arriving in Oman

On 15 March 2003, I waved goodbye to my family in Clontarf and headed out to the airport on the first stage of my journey to Oman. At Heathrow I treated myself to some smoked salmon and a couple of glasses of white wine being naïvely unaware that although Oman was a Muslim country, I was never going to have a problem getting a drink. The Gulf Air flight to Oman was quite empty – I think people were genuinely scared of travelling to the region with tensions so high.

I arrived in Muscat early the next morning; it was an amazing experience, landing with the sea on one side of the runway and the desert on the other. I collected my bags and walked to the arrivals hall where I was warmly greeted by Jim Flannery, the IDI project leader. We drove the 25 km from the airport into the centre of Muscat to the Sheraton Hotel, my home for the next couple of weeks until my apartment was ready. Oman was completely unlike anywhere else I'd ever been. Highways were edged with grass verges and beautiful flowers were tended to by Indian workers. Just feet away was the arid desert, contrasting with the flowers and the green of the continuous lawn along the roadside. Villas and houses were painted white and surrounded by large walls covered in bougainvillea.

The Sheraton Hotel was directly opposite the Department of Commerce and Industry, where I would be working for the next fifteen months. I showered and climbed into bed and slept soundly until woken by the phone ringing.

I was aware of the ringing, but I was suffering from a disorientating mixture of jetlag and tiredness that comes from sitting on an aeroplane seat all night. It was Jim: 'Because of what's happening in Iraq, the Saint Patrick's Day Ball has been cancelled, but our friend Terry is having a party in her house tonight and you're invited.'

I was about to excuse myself but then thought that I should make the effort, so I accepted the invitation. Jim picked me up later that evening and introduced me to his wife, Margaret, a charming woman from County Kerry. Their kindness and support made such a difference to my time in Oman, and they remain friends to this day.

Saint Patrick's Day

We drove to a suburb a few kilometres west of Muscat and stopped outside a large two-storey villa with dozens of cars and 4X4s parked outside. I could hear Irish music coming from behind the high walls but I wasn't prepared for the scene that greeted me when I walked into the garden.

A noisy Irish-style Saint Patrick's Day party was in full swing. There was bacon and cabbage and pints of Guinness being pulled by Indian waiters from the Sheraton Hotel. A bevy of young girls in Irish dancing costumes were getting ready to perform jigs and reels. This was all happening outdoors under the stars on a balmy March evening. What a contrast to the cold and damp weather I'd left twenty-four hours earlier.

I was introduced to members of the small but active Irish community and made to feel very welcome. Our hostess, Terry, was a remarkable woman married to a genial Iraqi. Being confined to a wheelchair had done nothing to suppress her energy and sense of fun; she was the glue that bound the Irish community together. Terry was forever organising social and community events to raise money for Omani charities. My first day in Oman had been unlike anything I'd ever experienced; my preconceived ideas of what it would be like were partly vindicated but in the most part they were shattered.

Starting work

The next day was Friday, and government offices and businesses were closed for the Muslim weekend, so I spent some time at the hotel pool. I got up for work early on Saturday morning, put on a long-sleeved white shirt and tie and suit, which was my work uniform from Saturday to Wednesday. The objective of the IDI project in Oman was to support ministry officials in devising a tourism development and marketing strategy that would allow Oman to grow tourism without becoming another Dubai.

The long-term objective was to lessen the dependency on oil revenues through the creation of a sustainable tourism industry, without selling out the rich cultural and social values that made Oman such a very special place.

I soon settled into my role as tourism marketing advisor, working in an office with Jim and two young Omani women, Hanadi and Razan.

Jackie's visit

A few weeks after my arrival, Jackie came on holiday, and during her stay we were invited to parties and social events. Jackie was invited to one of the weekly Mná na hÉireann social get-togethers organised by the Irish women living in Muscat. The introductions made there made it easier for her to settle in when she arrived in November to join me for five months.

Jackie and Frankincense tree.

Turtles

During Jackie's first visit we drove to Ras El Hadd, a small town named after a headland about 140 km east of Muscat. The area is famous for its beaches where thousands of Ridley turtles lay their eggs. The four-hour drive from Muscat was mostly on two-lane highway through desert terrain and occasional villages surrounded by date groves. These plantations were irrigated by underground springs fed by an ancient system of narrow stone channels called *falajs* that distributed the scarce water equitably to small holdings. Omnipresent were mountains of grey and black rocks scarred by wind and rain over the millennia. In many places engineers had blasted a roadway through the mountains, cutting miles off the journey.

Towards the end of the journey, we had to turn off the main highway and onto a smaller dirt road. The map was vague, but I was confident that if we drove due east, we'd get back onto the coast road. The light was fading, the dirt roads were now mostly sand, and we had to stop a couple of times to avoid camels. I began thinking that we'd end up having to sleep in the jeep but just before sunset, we saw some lights in the distance, the tar road started again. It was then another hour before we arrived at the newly opened Ras El Hadd Hotel, built among sand dunes about 3 km outside the town.

After a quick dinner we drove to the entrance of the nature reserve, where we joined a small group of visitors and a guide for our visit to the turtle hatching beach.

We were able to stand less than a metre from a huge turtle laying dozens of large eggs and using her flippers to cover them with sand. We also saw newly hatched babies emerge from under the sand and make their way to the sea. Baby turtles are victims of attacks by desert foxes, and crows and fewer than one in 1,000 to one in 10,000 reach adulthood. Interactions with humans are also a problem.

Newly hatched turtles are hardwired to crawl towards the white foam of waves breaking on the beach, but many on them crawled inland, confused by the white lights of the nearby hotel. It was heart-breaking to see hundreds of baby turtles squashed in the car park.

Visitors

During my time in Oman there was a steady stream of visitors. My daughters, Amy and Elaine, both came to stay, as did Jackie's sister, Tonya, and her husband, Stein; they lived in Norway so a trip to guaranteed winter sunshine was a bonus. Having a large penthouse apartment meant we had plenty of room for family and friends who came to stay.

We also had a couple of unexpected visitors. The late Tom Tescher, an Australian friend from my student travel days was visiting Oman as part of a so-called 'fam trip'. Fam trip is travel-speak for a familiarisation visit by overseas tour operators to persuade them to include Oman in their holiday brochures. I'd know Tom since his days of living in Thailand and managing the AUSTS student travel office in Bangkok. When the official part of the fam trip was over, Tom came to stay with us for a few days. He was always a pioneer, and I was glad to hear that his travel agency is still sending tourists to Oman.

Christmas lunch 2003 hosted by Denise and Doug Norris.

Into the desert

Our Canadian friends, Janet and Rod Hurd, and our daughter Amy came to stay in February, and we used their visit as an excuse for an overnight trip to the Wahiba Sands desert about 185 km from Muscat. We left the main road close to a town called Al Wasil and followed a dirt road to the nomadic desert camp. Accommodation was in spartan two-person rooms, though there was no need for air conditioning as it got surprisingly cool at night. The facilities were basic, and we had to check for scorpions before putting on our shoes. There were dune-bashing quad-bike rides but mostly it was just about soaking up the desert experience.

With my Omani colleagues in Musandam

Musandam

I had many wonderful experiences in Oman. Shortly after I arrived, Jim and I accompanied the ministry undersecretary and other officials on a one-night trip to the Musandam Governorate located on a mountainous peninsula projecting into the Strait of Hormuz.

Musandam has no land border with Oman, being separated by the United Arab Emirates, so we flew on Oman Air to the main town, Khasab. We were given a tour, which included a visit to a small harbour. I was curious about the large number of small narrow boats with enormous, long-shaft outboard motors that were moored there. Our guide explained that most nights these high-speed boats crossed the 34 km Strait of Hormuz, smuggling cigarettes to Iran and live goats back to Musandam.

At the time of my visit there were no suitable hotels in Khasab for our delegation, so we overnighted on a traditional dhow, which was anchored in a spectacular fjord-like inlet called a khor. After dinner on board, we sat on deck and chatted into the wee hours – magic.

Frankincense

Another great trip with Jackie was to the southern city of Salalah, on the coast about 600 km north of border with Yemen. Located in Dhofar Governate, Salalah and its environs have a rich archaeological heritage. The desert there is dotted with withered-looking frankincense trees (more like bushes), a reminder that Dhofar was at the centre of the valuable frankincense trade since the second century BC.

The legendary Queen of Sheba, who some believe ruled this region in the tenth century BC, is said to have built her summer palace there. Frankincense is still in daily use; the reception desk of my office in Muscat had a small pottery frankincense burner, which created aromatic fumes similar to those used to bless the deceased at Catholic funerals.

Job's tomb

An interesting side trip from Salalah was a visit to the tomb of the Prophet Job, mentioned in the Bible. The tomb itself was long and narrow, and while it was of religious significance it was housed in a modest small building. When we were there, we noticed a poster on the back wall depicting a stylised tree. On closer examination it turned out to be a family tree not only depicting Job's lineage but including Maria (Mary) and Jesus.

The khareef

Each year from late June until the end of August, the Dhofar region has a mini rainy season, the *khareef,* created by a monsoon that develops over the Arabian Sea. Almost overnight the arid landscape turns into a carpet of green. Visitors from all over the Middle East and Gulf visit Salalah to escape the searing heat and to spend time in the cool foggy greenery. Coming from Ireland, we scratched our heads wondering why anyone would pay to sit in the rain.

For a few weeks the Khareef monsoon turns southern Oman green.

CHAPTER 39

Moldova, 2004

Air Moldova

The project in Moldova was managed by my friend Derek O'Brien on behalf of the EU. It focused on the providing the EU with an overview of the commercial viability of Air Moldova, which was struggling to compete in a post-Aeroflot world.

We stayed in the Soviet-era Cosmos Hotel in the centre of the capital, Chisinau, and travelled each morning to the airline's offices at the airport.

The commercial director of Air Moldova was competent and had progressive ideas, but the general director was a state appointee who seemed happy with the status quo. Our work was hindered by the fact that the general director essentially refused to engage with us, citing having to attend 'very important meetings' as an excuse for not meeting us.

Challenges

Moldova, formerly part of the Soviet Union, is one of Europe's poorest countries and home to 2.6 million people. Its economic salvation is that many Moldovans speak Romanian and qualify for Romanian passports, allowing them to work in the EU.

The country is landlocked, surrounded by Ukraine and Romania. On its eastern border lies the breakaway region of Transnistria, with a predominantly Russian-speaking population that Moscow has supported for decades. These are just some of the factors that explain why Moldova has failed to attract foreign investment.

Air Moldova lurched from crisis to crisis and faced competition from private airlines but at the time of writing it is still operating.

CHAPTER 40

Iran, 2004

In the early 2000s the International Student Travel Confederation (ISTC) engaged with student representative associations in Iran with a view to expanding the distribution of the International Student Identity Card (ISIC). This dialogue culminated the student association of the University of Tehran inviting an ISTC delegation to visit Iran.

During my time working for USIT I was responsible for expanding the range of student discounts for ISIC card holders, including the popular CIE Travelsave scheme for public transport discounts. The ISTC invited me to join their delegation so that I could share my experiences in Ireland and offer advice on launching the ISIC in Iran.

The first hurdle was to get an Iranian visa, and that involved a visit and interview in the Iranian Embassy on Mount Merrion Avenue in Blackrock. The officials there were curious about my visit, but once my credentials were verified, I was issued a visa. I travelled to Iran in mid-2004 but there are no entry or exit stamps or visa in my passport to record my visit.

Tehran

The ISTC delegation was headed up by the ISTC CEO David Jones, whom I met at Schiphol Airport in Amsterdam, and we flew together on a KLM flight to Tehran. On arrival we were met at the steps of the aircraft and escorted to a VIP area, where we waited for our passports to be processed and our baggage delivered to us.

The stunning 17th-century Imam (Shah) Mosque, Isfahan.

We stayed in a nice hotel near the university and had a couple of days of meetings and briefings. Tehran itself was a sprawling city criss-crossed with elevated motorways; the only remarkable features were the huge building-sized murals depicting freedom fighters and imagery depicting the US as Satan.

Isfahan

Having completed the formal part of the visit David and I were invited to spend a night in the beautiful city of Isfahan, located about 441 km south of the capital.

At the centre of Isfahan was Naqsh-e Jahan Square, built in the early 1600s, which had at one end the stunning Shah Mosque, a UNESCO World Heritage Site. The outside of the mosque had a collage of beautiful blue tiles – it was one of the most beautiful places that I'd been.

Buying a rug

When David and I were strolling around the square with our guide, we somehow ended up in a carpet shop owned, surprise, surprise, by our guide's cousin.

We were sat down, served tea and shown a selection of rugs. Neither of us really needed a rug but we got the impression that we were not going to be let leave without making a purchase. I pleaded that I had a small suitcase (and a small house) and I could only carry a small rug. After some haggling, I eventually bought a beautiful small silk rug. David was talked into buying a larger one.

Iran Air

When it came time to return to Tehran, I opted to fly rather than face another long car journey. I took a taxi to the airport, checked in and waited in the departure lounge. I was clearly a foreigner, and a number of people approached me and asked if I needed any help. The Iran Air flight was operated by an old Boeing 727 with the original 1970s interior; American sanctions meant that it was very difficult for the airline to purchase new equipment or spares. During the short flight I was served a snack, juice and tea. All in all, it was a surprisingly pleasant experience.

CHAPTER 41

Zambezi Airlines, Zambia, 2008

Having worked most of my consultancy life in Eastern Europe and the former Soviet Union, I had never worked on a big project in sub-Saharan Africa.

That all changed on in early May 2008. It was glorious early-summer day, and I was in the middle of Lough Owel fishing. My friend Stephen Feldman had just hooked a trout when my mobile rang. The caller identified himself as a representative of Zambezi Airlines and added that he had been told to contact me regarding setting up an airline in Zambia. The call quality was poor, and the noise of the wind and waves meant I was not able to understand much of the conversation.

When I got back to Dublin, I called the gentleman, who I now know as Jomo Matululu, who explained that his boss had leased a twenty-nine-seat aircraft and wanted to launch an airline in early July. It became clear that except for the aircraft and pilots, the airline had very little else in place.

To break the communications impasse, I offered to travel to Lusaka the next week and spend a few days there on a scoping exercise to see what was required and to make a consultancy proposal. I explained that there was no

Hippos - Zambezi River 17.6.2012

charge for the scoping exercise, but the airline would be expected to arrange a prepaid return ticket from Dublin and to pay my hotel and other expenses while I was in Zambia. We agreed that I would travel the following Monday but when the ticket didn't arrive by lunchtime, I concluded that the deal was off. However, shortly afterwards I received an e-ticket for a British Airways flight that evening and off I went.

When I arrived in Lusaka, I was met by Jomo and taken to the Intercontinental Hotel and later that afternoon I met the chairman, Maurice Jangulo, who told me that the inaugural flight was planned for about six weeks' time in mid-July.

Making a plan

My first cultural acclimatisation experience was the next morning when I was picked up by Jomo. I asked about the schedule for my trip, and he said, 'We'll make a plan.' I soon learned to treat those words more as an aspiration than reality; what they really meant was making a plan about making a plan.

When I visited the airline's temporary office in the Crismar Hotel. I realised the challenge that I faced. Except for an engineering manager, chief pilot and a couple of people who had worked for the now-defunct national airline, there was nobody with experience of modern airline operations.

I identified that the airline would need a reservation system, branding, aircraft livery, signage, an email server, a phone system, airport and city ticket offices, a website, an online payment system, uniforms, marketing collateral, a schedule, on-board catering, and access to the travel agent distribution systems – and all this by the planned inaugural flight less than two months later.

I gave the chairman a consultancy proposal, which he accepted, and I set about helping Zambezi Airlines become a reality. I enjoyed those hectic start-up days and gradually put together a commercial department team, which felt like Yul Brynner assembling the Magnificent Seven.

Branding

I needed a brand identity for the airline that reflected its Zambian roots but would be neutral enough to use in other markets. My eureka moment came when I was walking towards the lift in the Intercontinental Hotel.

The walls were decorated with lithographs of stylised animals, including a giraffe. I remembered that Zambia was home to Thornicroft's giraffe, so I briefed Des Kiely, a graphic designer friend in Ireland, and within a few days he presented a layout for stationery, signage and, most importantly, the livery for the Boeing 737s.

Inaugural flight

The inaugural flight from Lusaka to Livingstone took place on 15 July 2008. There were VIPs and dignitaries on board and I remained in Lusaka Airport to oversee the press conference and reception that was planned for when the flight returned. As is the norm for most inaugural flights, this one was almost an hour late arriving back in Lusaka. The airport manager provided the VIP suite, and there were speeches and toasts to Zambia's newest airline. As the only mzungu (white person) present I stood discretely at the back of the room, and I was surprised and embarrassed when the chairman singled me out for his thanks and a round of applause.

Because there was only one aircraft, the start-up schedule was limited to a few domestic destinations, notably Livingstone (Victoria Falls) and Ndola.

Expansion

Later that year the chairman, Dr Jangulo, began discussions with Irish leasing company GE Capital Aviation Services, and a few weeks later the airline took delivery of two Boeing 737-500 aircraft with twelve business-class and 120 economy seats. My challenge was to arrange landing slots at OR Tambo International Airport in Johannesburg, set up ground-handling agreements and arrange catering in both Lusaka and Johannesburg.

The first international route to Johannesburg began on 12 May 2009, followed shortly afterwards by flights to Dar es Salaam. Very soon the airline gained a reputation for on-board service and reliability.

One of the proudest moments of my aviation career was to watch the pilots and cabin crew walking across the ramp wearing uniforms that I'd helped design to the stunning-looking Zambezi Airlines aircraft being provisioned with catering that I'd organised.

Kenneth Kaunda

In early December 2009 I was returning to Dublin from Lusaka via Johannesburg. Our daughter Elaine had completed her Bachelor of Nursing course in Trinity College and was graduating the next morning. I boarded the Lusaka to Jo'burg flight and sat in seat 1A, the first row of business class.

Departure time approached, passengers were boarded, and I was sure we'd push back on time. The cabin supervisor told me that we were delayed waiting for a VIP and she asked me to move to the aisle seat. 'Sure, no problem,' I said. The VIP sitting in my window seat was Dr Kenneth Kaunda, the first President of Zambia, accompanied by two bodyguards.

I feel privileged for the opportunity to spend two hours sitting next to one of the last of the post-colonial leaders. He was a very entertaining and knowledgeable travelling companion and told me of his friendship with our former president, Mary Robinson. He was curious about me and what I was doing in Zambia. I explained that I had been helping Zambezi Airlines and I was travelling back to Ireland to attend my daughter's graduation in TCD.

On a whim I ripped a page out of my A5 diary, and asked Dr Kaunda if he would mind writing a short note to Elaine. He said he'd be delighted and seemed happy to be asked. His message was warm and gracious and it's framed together with Elaine's graduation certificate as a memory of that occasion. As we disembarked in Johannesburg one of his bodyguards leaned over and said to me, 'Thanks for looking after the boss.'

By 2010 I became worried that the airline was expanding very rapidly without sufficient planning or funding. I expressed by concerns to the chairman but the strategy didn't change and so I felt the only option was to terminate our agreement. Somewhat predictably the airline ceased operations in November 2011.

CHAPTER 42

Montserrat, 2009

Island man

Since by first consultancy project I seem to have gravitated towards islands, most of them tiny and in out-of-the way places. My assignment in Montserrat was unique in that it was the smallest island I'd visited and the smallest with its own airline.

Montserrat is a British overseas territory in the British West Indies approximately 50 km from Antigua; it's small, just 16 km long and 11 km wide, and about half the island is an exclusion zone because of a volcanic eruption in 1995.

Emerald Isle

Montserrat is also known as the Emerald Isle because many of Montserrat's residents have Irish ancestry. It's the only country outside of Ireland to designate Saint Patrick's Day as a national holiday. Montserrat's residents with Irish ancestry have names like Farrell, Kirwan, Roche, O'Donoghue, Lynch, Sweeney and Ryan. While they celebrate Saint Patrick's Day and their immigration stamp includes a shamrock, I got the impression that they didn't know that much about Ireland.

Montserrat Airways

I met my client, Captain Nigel Harris, socially when he ran an airline in the UK. He later moved to live on Montserrat and started Montserrat Airways. He contacted me about setting up an online booking engine and website, and I was delighted to take the assignment even though the finances weren't great. It was a chance for me to visit that part of the world.

Getting to Montserrat

I flew from Gatwick to Antigua and waited a couple of hours for the connecting flight to Montserrat. The airline had only two aircraft, both twin-engine nine-seat Britten-Norman Islanders, which were suitable for the short runway on Montserrat. The same type of aircraft still link the Aran Islands with an airstrip in Inverin on the Galway mainland.

Olveston House once owned by Beatles producer Sir George Martin.

The Beatles connection

Nigel had booked me into the Olveston House hotel, once owned by the Beatles producer, Sir George Martin. It was leased to two charming Irish American women from Boston on the proviso that he would take back the house for the month of January each year. As I was the only guest, I was given 'Paul's Room', he of Beatles fame. The hall corridor was decorated with beautiful original black and white photos taken by Linda McCarthy.

In 1979 George Martin set up the AIR recording studios in Montserrat so artists could be somewhere with no distractions; apparently many of

Original photos by Linda McCartney

the locals didn't even recognise the big names like Sting. Many iconic albums were recorded in the AIR studio until 1989, when Hurricane Hugo hit the island and caused extensive damage, forcing Martin to close the studios.

Volcanic activity

In 1997 volcanic eruptions destroyed Montserrat's capital, Plymouth, and the airport. Since then, there's been low-level volcanic activity, which I experienced first-hand on one of my visits. I was awoken by what I thought was thunder, but there was no lightning or rain squalls. I stepped onto my bedroom balcony to investigate and was shocked to see the volcano gently rumbling away. Nobody else in the hotel seemed concerned, so I went back to bed. I mentioned my experience to the manager next morning and she was almost dismissive: 'Ah, that was nothing. It's often far scarier.'

Border control, island style

For such a small place, border control on Montserrat made arriving in the UK seem like a breeze. I arrived from Antigua with six other passengers, all locals. I was sitting in the back row of the Islander aircraft and by the time I scrambled over the seats to disembark, the other passengers were already in the small terminal.

When I got to the immigration hall, I was alone. I presented my passport to the officer on duty and was told I'd need to complete an arrivals form. I handed him the completed form and he proceeded to quiz me on why I was in Montserrat, asking where was I going to stay and for how long. Having determined I was not a terrorist operative, he stamped my passport with a lovely shamrock-shaped arrival stamp (Fáilte Ireland, take note).

I thanked him and walked to collect my bag and headed for the customs green channel, only to find the same official waiting to greet me, this time in his role as customs officer. He quizzed me about the contents of my bag and asked me to open it for a quick check. Here was a man who took his job seriously.

Bush Rum

Nigel met me outside and suggested we have a drink at the airport bar, nestled under the roof of the terminal but otherwise open to the elements. The bar was hopping with locals having a few Friday-evening drinks.

Nigel and I squeezed onto a couple of stools at the counter right next to the multitasking officer who introduced himself and became our amiable drinking companion. Nigel insisted I sample Bush Rum, local hooch served on ice with Tang as a mixer; Tang is a 1950s-era orange-flavoured drink that seems to still be a big seller in the Caribbean.

I added the Tang, toasted my host, took a sip, and then almost hit the roof. It was like drinking an aromatic, exotic version of poitín. Later in the evening I has coming back from the loo and happened to see the barman adding twigs and jugs of liquid into a large plastic container that looked like rubbish bin.

It was only when I ordered another round of drinks that I saw our order being decanted from the same bin under the counter.

Bush Rum was a blend of leaves, bark, twigs and roots added to overproof rum and which supposedly had medicinal benefits. Having woken up with a throbbing headache, I can attest that curing hangovers is not one of those benefits.

CHAPTER 43

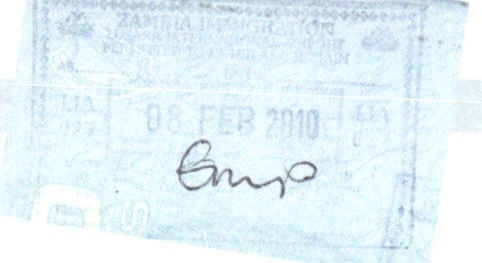

Proflight Zambia, 2010

When I finished my assignment with Zambezi Airlines I was approached by Keira Irwin, the commercial director of Proflight Zambia, and asked to evaluate several reservation systems because the homegrown system they were using was no longer fit for purpose.

Having reviewed several vendors, I recommended Videcom, a UK-based system that required very limited internet bandwidth. My recommendation was accepted, and I was then asked to project manage the implementation of the system.

When that project was completed, I was tasked with helping Proflight join the two major global distribution systems, Galileo and Amadeus. These systems allowed travel agents around the world make real-time reservations and issue tickets. To facilitate the associated financial transactions, Proflight also joined the IATA Bank Settlement Plan and the IATA Clearing House

From that point onwards Proflight morphed from being a small quasi-charter, quasi-scheduled airline to one focusing on the development of a domestic and regional flight network.

My role transitioned from one-off project work to a more long-term role as advisor/mentor focusing on the commercial side of the business. During my time with Proflight I had the opportunity to hop on a plane and spend weekends in the bush at one of the many safari camps and lodges along the Lower Zambezi River or South Luangwa National Park.

One of my happy places was Flatdogs Camp in South Luangwa National Park. During the first few grim months of Covid lockdown I often fantasied about going out on an early morning game drive, breathing in the cool dawn air and savouring the magical smell of the bush.

My enduring memory of Zambia is the warmth of people I met and worked with there, whether be it chatting to a taxi driver, being the only mzungu sitting at a bar counter or in the office. I'm especially grateful for my relationship with the extended Irwin family, with whom I had both a professional and personal relationship. The Proflight CEO, Tony Irwin, set up the airline in 1991, and thirty-two years later it is still in business (and growing), making it unique in terms of private airlines in Africa.

Lubumbashi

During my time with Proflight I was often entrusted with what I call 'missionary work', including setting up a short-lived route from Lusaka to Lubumbashi, formerly Élisabethville, in the Democratic Republic of Congo, and a fact-finding trip to Mozambique.

The trip to Lubumbashi threw up some surprises, such as the presence of large Greek community and a synagogue. The back story is that in 1911, Sephardic Jews came from Rhodes, then part of the Ottoman Empire, and settled in Lubumbashi. The Greeks followed when their former neighbours reported business opportunities in the then Belgian Congo.

CHAPTER 44

Mozambique, 2012

I went to Mozambique in 2012 not really knowing what to expect. Wearing my 'John the Baptist' hat, Proflight had tasked me with scoping out the demand for flights from Mozambique to Zambia.

Despite being Portuguese-speaking and having an AK47 and Marxist symbols on its national flag, Mozambique is a member of the Commonwealth of Nations. It joined in 1995 and at the time was unique in that it did not having a historic constitutional relationship with the United Kingdom or speak English.

The Irish Embassy in Mozambique was helpful in terms of setting up meetings with tour operators, travel agents, the Ministry of Tourism, etc. They also booked my hotel, the Southern Sun, right on the beach yet convenient to Maputo city centre. Much of the architecture in Maputo reminded me of Eastern Europe with its grandiose Soviet-era public buildings and parks.

The road to my hotel ran parallel to sand dunes, and every few hundred metres there were beach bars, cafés, and restaurants, one of which was a short walk from the hotel. The hall porter assured me it was a safe area, so I walked to a local restaurant, Sagres, which would not have looked out of place on any small Mediterranean beachfront. I was given a table and began the evening with a cold 2M beer: a nice easy name if you don't speak Portuguese.

Some tables close by were being pushed together to form one long table, which waiters were setting up for a party of about thirty people: a celebration dinner of some kind. Guests started to arrive with large bunches of flowers, which were given to the bartenders to be placed in jugs and vases on the table. It reminded me of the same practice in Ukraine and I wondered if it was a legacy from the time when Mozambique had a socialist regime supported by the Soviet Union.

One of the guests told me they were celebrating their grandmother's eightieth birthday, so I asked him to pass on my best wishes to her. This he did and the old lady turned to me, smiled said something in Portuguese and I was immediately invited to join their table for a drink and to share their celebrations.

The last part of my trip involved flying north to place called Tete, a small city on the Zambezi River, close to the Malawi and Zambian borders. It was a hot, unremarkable place with the dubious distinction of being the site of one of the largest open-cast coal mines in the world. Given its relative proximity to Lusaka, the plan was to start a route from Tete to Lusaka with connections to other parts of the world. I met with a number of travel agents, who predicted that there would be a market for a scheduled flight to Lusaka, but there was no data to support that view. The deteriorating economic situation and jihadist insurgency in the north caused the project to be abandoned.

At the end of my stay, Proflight sent a four-seat aircraft to fly me directly back to Lusaka rather than have me go the 'long way round' via Maputo and Johannesburg.

CHAPTER 45

Kenya, 2014

Most of my projects start with an out-the-blue email or phone call, and my engagement by Fly540 was no different. Fly540 started operations between Nairobi and Mombasa in November 2006, and the airline's name refers to KSh5,540 – the adult return fare at the time.

The airline was founded by Don Smith, a larger-than-life Liverpudlian with an innate entrepreneurial flair and a 'robust' negotiating style.

In March 2014 I was hired to do a one-week review of the airline's commercial department, focusing on marketing and distribution. At the end of the week, I made a presentation, which was well received even though it included some criticism of the organisational culture and management style.

My point of contact in the airline was the finance director, Rob Davidson, who also owned the Purdy Arms pub and guest house, where I stayed during my visits to Nairobi. Rob lived on site, so I travelled to and from the office with him.

The Purdy Arms was a once a large colonial-era family home, located on extensive grounds in the posh Nairobi suburb of Karen, named after Karen Blixen, whose life and book inspired the movie *Out of Africa*. The bar in the Purdy Arms was patronised mostly by expatriate types, a cohort of whom occupied the same bar stools every evening. They were good company and straight of Central Casting for *Out of Africa*.

A few days before one of my trips I got a phone call from Rob telling me that the Purdy Arms had been robbed the previous weekend by a small gang of men with Kalashnikovs. While nobody was hurt, he offered me the option of staying in a nearby hotel. I declined the offer, and by way of reassurance he explained security guards were patrolling the grounds at night.

My flight from London arrived after 10 p.m. and it was midnight by the time my taxi arrived at the guesthouse. Driving up the dark driveway, I saw nobody about; so much for the security. The taxi pulled up outside the guesthouse and as I waited for the driver to get my luggage, I was aware of shadowy figures appearing from the surrounding bushes. For a moment I thought it was another robbery, but in fact they were three Maasai warriors armed with spears, who escorted me to the hall door. It brought a whole new meaning to the term 'private security'.

Shortly after I had I returned to Dublin, I received a contract extension to negotiate the renewal of agreements with Travelport and Amadeus, and to do a forensic audit of financial reports from a ticketing partner in Europe.

Travelport and Amadeus, so-called GDS systems, provided travel agents with computer access that enabled agents to make bookings and issue tickets on Fly540 flights. Fly540 was a big customer of both GDSs, but Don was unhappy about their segment fees and the automatic annual fee increase built into the contract. He also disliked the clause that penalised the airline if it offered promotional fares – web fares that were not available from travel agents.

The relationship had become very toxic, with Fly540 threatening to cancel the agreements and sell exclusively online and through its own offices. For their part, the GDSs threatened legal injunctions to recover their debts.

The second part of my brief was to review the agreement with a company providing Fly540 with worldwide ticketing services. Their business model was to take a 9 per cent commission, deducted from payments to Fly540. When I forensically examined some of the remittances, not all the taxes paid by the passenger were being passed on to Fly540 Airlines.

The wording of the agreement and its interpretation prompted me to go back through historical records. Then began a series of emails and conference calls with the ticketing service where I argued that Fly540 was due a sizeable refund. These long-distance negotiations were going nowhere, so Don agreed that I should have a face-to-face meeting with the partner in their offices in Europe.

After about three hours of negotiations, we agreed a full and final settlement. As soon as I left the meeting, I phoned Don to tell him that a six-figure sum would be transferred to Fly540 the following week. He was very happy with the outcome.

Masai Mara

My trips to Nairobi typically involved a weekend, and on one such occasion Don asked, 'Where would you like to go for the weekend, bush or beach?'

I replied that I'd love to go to the bush. Within a few hours I was handed flight tickets and a voucher for two nights in a game lodge in the Masai Mara National Reserve, plus an envelope with a few thousand Kenyan Shillings as 'pocket money'.

Early the next morning I took a taxi to Wilson Airport, a 1930s-era airport on the edge of Nairobi. The airport was used by charter airlines to fly tourists to the numerous game lodges and safari camps in the Masai Mara National Reserve.

My flight was operated by Safarilink, using a twelve-seat Cessna Caravan aircraft. There were six other passengers: three honeymoon couples staying in different safari camps. The flight operated taxi style, droppings off passengers at different landing strips, one of which was only a five-minute flight from the previous one. I was dropped off last and met by a guide, who drove me to a very nice lodge.

The next morning, I headed out on a game drive with a driver and a Maasai guide. The Maasai people still wear their distinctive dress and have largely retained their cultural identity. Maasai are semi-nomadic and pastoral: they live by herding cattle, which form the basis of their diet and act as the measure of their wealth and status.

At the end of the weekend, I checked out of the lodge only to be told that my flight back to Nairobi would be delayed by two hours. The lodge manager kindly invited me to pass some time by having afternoon tea on the veranda. The chef was there making pancakes, watched over by a Maasai warrior with his spear, shield and full regalia.

The chef left briefly to go to the kitchen, and I said, half-jokingly, to the Maasai man that I would take over the pancake making.

'Oh man, oh man, you shouldn't be doing that sort of work,' he said, 'That's work for women.'

Winding him up, I explained that I often helped my wife with cooking and household chores such as peeling potatoes, ironing and cooking dinner.

He looked shell-shocked and went off muttering, 'Oh man, oh man.'

Out of Africa

When in Nairobi I arranged to visit the one-time home of Karen Blixen, the Danish woman who travelled alone from Denmark to Kenya in 1914 to marry her fiancé and set up a dairy farm. By the time she arrived, her husband had changed his mind about keeping cattle and they became coffee farmers. Her fascinating story was the inspiration for the 1985 movie *Out of Africa*, starring Robert Redford as Denys Hatton, a local big-game hunter with whom she had an intimate relationship. Meryl Streep played Karen Blixen in the movie. Her house, once in a rural area, was now in an outer suburb of Nairobi, close to my guest house. The house has been faithfully preserved as a museum.

I learned that Karen Blixen was an accomplished artist who had studied at the Royal Danish Academy of Fine Arts in Copenhagen. She painted portraits of several of her servants, including Farah, a Somali who became her friend and confidant. I bought a few A1 size reproductions and had them framed.

Outside Karen Blixen's house near Nairobi, now a museum.

Fly540 closes

In November 2022 the Competition Authority of Kenya ordered Fly540 to cease operations following customer complaints about flight cancellations and revelations that its operating certificate had recently expired. I've no doubt that Don will, like every true Scouser, come back to fight another day.

CHAPTER 46

Sardinia, 2014

My time in Sardinia working for Meridiana Airlines and its successor, Air Italy, was one of the most rewarding of my consultancy career.

Back story

It started in early December 2014, when Dick Creagh invited me to his holiday home in Mountshannon, on the shores of Lough Derg. Dick was a former senior executive of Aer Lingus and deputy president of Ukraine International Airlines. We'd worked on several projects, including mystery traveller customer service audits at European airports served by Ukraine International.

Over dinner Dick explained that he had been shortlisted for a turnaround project with Meridiana Airlines, with the objective of stopping the losses and identifying potential investors.

Meridiana's predecessor, Alisarda was founded in 1963 by the Aga Khan, leader of the Nizari Ismaili Shias and one of the richest men in the world. The Aga Khan was responsible for developing several up-market tourism projects on the Costa Smeralda coast of Sardinia. The state airline, Alitalia, was unable or unwilling to increase their schedule to Olbia, which prompted the Aga Khan to start his own airline.

Against stiff competition Dick was awarded the contract and began the project the following week. I was delighted to get a call from Dick asking if I could 'come down to Olbia for a week to take a look at the commercial side of the airline'.

Olbia

The week before Christmas I flew to Rome and took the late-evening connecting flight to Olbia. The highway into town was lined with neat grass verges and flowering shrubs. Olbia itself was a pleasant town decked out with Christmas decorations, but I was surprised at how quiet it was. Sardinia is a very seasonal tourist destination, and between November and March many restaurants and hotels are closed.

When I'd finished my week, I returned to Dublin thinking that was the end of my involvement, but over Christmas I got a call from Dick asking if I could commit to a longer contract. I said yes, we agreed terms, and I travelled back to Olbia early in 2015.

There were two terminals at Olbia Airport – one for scheduled flights and the other, equally large, a general aviation terminal. Between October and June there were relatively few charter flights or business jets using the general aviation terminal, but during July and August there were literally dozens of aircraft parked nose to nose on the tarmac. In addition to the normal executive jets there were commercial jets such as Boeing 767s and Airbus 330s.

These larger aircraft were typically owned by the royal families of Gulf States who spent the summer in their villas on Sardinia's north coast. Their entourage included extended family, maids, cooks and other staff. The flight crews are expected to stay in Olbia and be on standby for an unexpected departure.

My role

My role was to both reduce costs and improve customer service standards. I helped the airline renegotiate contracts, but improving the customer experience proved trickier. Meridiana operated a fleet of aging aircraft, including the last MD-80s and B767s, which were prone to technical problems. Punctuality and schedule integrity were poor, which resulted in complaints and claims under EU consumer protection legislation. Together with colleagues we worked on improving the airport and on-board experience.

Naples

As part of my brief, I visited several Italian airports to audit the customer experience. Most memorable was my visit to Naples, which, to many of my colleagues, was bandit country and not really part of Italy. They couldn't understand why I would ever want to go there.

Meridiana was the only airline offering direct flights from New York to Naples, which made it especially popular with the aging 'Soprano's' market, who liked the convenience of a direct flight from JFK.

The flights were heavily booked all summer, and the passenger demographic presented some unusual challenges. Boarding took longer than usual and there more wheelchair requests than normal – on the flight I observed being boarded there were over fifty wheelchairs.

New investor

While the various cost-saving and revenue-generating initiatives helped, the longer-term strategy was to find an investor, preferably another airline. Several options were explored and eventually Qatar Airways agreed to become a shareholder in what seemed to be a sweetheart deal to save the airline and avoid bankruptcy. Within a few weeks Meridiana was rebranded as Air Italy, the first A330 aircraft arrived from Qatar Airways to replace the aging B767s and the airline announced new routes.

Qatar Airways insisted that the consultancy and most senior management contracts be terminated and replaced by their own team.

AviaPay

Under the circumstances I was sorry to lose my contract, but thankfully this was not the end of my relationship with Air Italy. Working with software partners in South Africa, I developed a point-of-sale app called AviaPay. The application was designed so that low-cost airlines could take payment for on-board sales of drinks and snacks. The first customer, FlySafair in South Africa, purchased over a hundred devices.

The original app had been designed for in-flight use, but with a few tweaks it worked in the less challenging terrestrial environment. Air Italy used the device to collect excess baggage fees at their check-in counters, initially in Milan Malpensa Airport but later in Rome Fiumicino Airport.

The usual procedure involved passengers being sent to the ticket desk at the far end of the terminal, waiting in a queue, paying, and then making their way back to check in. But with the AviaPay machine, the check-in agent could process the sale, take payment and issue a printed receipt within a couple of minutes. In the first six months of the trial, Meridiana collected over €500,000 in excess baggage and other ancillary charges. In early February 2020 they told me they wanted to deploy AviaPay at JFK and other long-haul destinations.

Air Italy bankruptcy

11 February 2020 was a significant day. I was composing an offer to Air Italy for the rental of devices to use at JFK, but the proposal was never sent, and the email remains in my archive folder. The reason? that afternoon I received an email announcing that Air Italy had gone into liquidation with immediate effect, and a liquidator had been appointed.

It would be simplistic to blame Covid for the demise of Air Italy; the reasons go a lot deeper and include unrealistic demands from trade unions and rumours that Air Italy was paying above market lease rates on the new aircraft. We'll never know if a stronger Air Italy would have survived Covid; probably not.

Over the following couple of weeks, I received payment for outstanding device rentals and the twenty devices were delivered back to me.

I enjoyed everything about my time working in Sardinia: the ladies at the café in the airport terminal who giggled at my attempts to order lunch in Italian; not having to order my favourite tipple in the bar of the Jazz Hotel, the kindness and patience of people when I used crutches, and the many missteps I made trying to order dinner from the Italian menu.

My consultancy career started on the island of Aruba, and I've worked in many other islands since then – maybe I'll get one final gig on Zanzibar?

View of Olbia Airport from my office.

CHAPTER 47

Madeira, 2020

Jackie and I arrived in Madeira on 1 November 2020. This was the culmination of an idea that began out of feelings of depression in the early months of Covid lockdown and ended with us deplaning into warm Madeira sunshine.

Surviving lockdown

We coped well at the start of Covid, although the images coming out of Northern Italy were distressing. My survival strategy was to go out on my bike early every morning and cycle diligently designed circular routes that kept me within 2 km of home. During May 2020 I began getting up a 5.30 a.m., and armed with a flask of coffee, I'd cycle up to the end of the Bull Island Causeway and home via Saint Anne's Park, where I'd stop for more coffee. I avoided contact with other early risers, and if the gardaí had a check point I'd get a friendly wave.

We started getting home deliveries of fresh fish and occasionally ready-cooked meals from Casa Clontarf. While supermarkets were open, there were limits on the number of people allowed inside, resulting in long queues. Being in a vulnerable age group, we opted to use the Tesco click-and-collect service. Jackie shopped online and chose a time slot for pick-up at a designated spot in the Tesco car park in Clare Hall.

I did some long-distance mentoring for Proflight Zambia, but when they were forced to suspend flights, I read a lot and kept in touch with friends using Zoom.

Isolate Bar

To stay connected with our neighbours, I set up my 'Isolate Bar' in the front garden. I designed a lawn sign to identify the bar, and while Jackie and I were the only customers, passing pedestrians would stop and have a socially-distanced chat from the street.

Escape planning

By July 2020 the omens were not looking good; it seemed like lockdowns and movement restrictions were going to continue into the winter. This triggered the idea of leaving Ireland and going somewhere with less Covid and warmer winter weather. Not only would this be a great adventure for us, but our daughter Elaine and her family could move into our house and stop paying for rented accommodation.

In mid-2020 New Zealand had almost zero Covid cases, and with Jackie's ancestral NZ passport we were both eligible to go there. Our first plan was to arrive in Auckland in early November and spend the next six months or a year travelling around the country. We then became concerned about the costs involved and the risk that New Zealand would close its borders. These factors forced us to rethink our plans and look for somewhere in Europe. But where?

Madeira

By July 2020 many European countries had closed their borders, and the testing requirements and public health rules seemed to change on a regular basis. I started to search for somewhere we could go in Europe and remembered that Madeira always promoted itself as the Island of Endless Springtime.

My research showed that Madeira had very few Covid cases, and the only restrictions were compulsory indoor mask-wearing and occasional curfews. Shops and restaurants were open, and warmer weather meant that outdoor dining was possible during the day.

Getting there involved an overnight in Heathrow, and we had to get the first of many PCR tests within forty-eight hours of travel.

First impressions

Our first impressions of Madeira were positive. Covid test checking at the airport was friendly and well organised; during a short wait in the screening queue, we were handed a bottle of cold water and a banana. During the fifteen-minute taxi journey to our apartment we were surprised to see flowers in bloom, palm trees and lots of banana plantations.

The welcome food pack we ordered was a little meagre, so we walked twenty minutes to the nearest town, Cancela, to get more supplies. We stocked up with some basics and walked back to our apartment. When we were passing a villa, we saw people in the garden harvesting fruit from a tree. I asked if they were mangos.

One of the men replied, 'No, they're avocados.'

We said our goodbyes, but a few minutes later we heard a call and turned to see one of the men walking towards us with the gift of an avocado.

The reception at the airport and the simple gift of an avocado were two small gestures that typified our seven months on Madeira. Whether it was interacting with staff at the vaccination centre or a waiter at a restaurant, we were made feel welcome at every turn.

Somewhere to live

From my research, and a lot of Google Earth fly passes, I saw that most of the tourist high-rise hotels and apartments were west of Funchal, the capital. We wanted somewhere with more character, and I managed to negotiate a six-month lease in the Palheiro Village resort, about 3 km east and high above Funchal. The apartment was spacious, with two bedrooms, a large living area and a balcony overlooking the ocean. Because we were so high above the sea, the horizon created a wide border between sea and sky.

While our apartment was super, the apartment village was almost empty of guests, so we had little or no contact with neighbours. Our salvation was the Number 38 bus, which passed the entrance of our complex on its way to and from Funchal. The bus service on Madeira is fantastic; what it lacked in frequency it made up for with to-the-minute punctuality.

Making friends

Our social life got a boost when our estate agent mentioned that she'd sold a house to a couple relocating from the Caribbean and that the woman was looking for a tennis partner. Jackie said that she was also looking for someone to play with, and she was introduced to Karen Wilson. They started to play in the nearby Casa Verde Hotel on at least a weekly basis, giving Jackie a 'date in the diary'. It was a bonus that the Wilsons had bought a villa close to our apartment.

I got to know Karen's husband, Barry, who was born in Rhodesia but travelled extensively during his career in the pharma industry and now lived between Geneva and Madeira. He was an aviation junky who kept a flight logbook since he'd started flying – an even bigger aviation nerd than me!

Barry and Karen were avid hillwalkers, and their relocation to Madeira was prompted by the temperate climate, good health care and Madeira's extensive network of walking trails along the old levada water channels.

View from our first apartment, Palheiro Village.

For the remainder of our time on Madeira, and on subsequent trips, we enjoyed many a pleasant lunch and dinner together, in local restaurants and in each other's houses.

Christmas

Our Christmas on Madeira was different from our usual family celebrations, and while we missed our family and traditions, we were determined to enjoy ourselves. On 7 December we took the ferry to Porto Santo, a small island about two hours by ferry from Funchal.

There are only 7,000 inhabitants on the island, and it was a sleepy sort of a place, but unlike Madeira it had a sandy beach.

We did some exploring, had a swim, ate lunch and sat on the beach, before taking the evening ferry back to Funchal.

Funchal City Council did a great job decorating the city with beautiful lights and cribs. Jackie made some decorations, I bought fairy lights and we made the apartment look very Christmassy. We had a swim on Christmas Eve and booked the Case Verde Hotel for Christmas dinner. Christmas Day was very wet and windy, so the hotel sent a car to collect us and drop us home afterwards.

New Year's Eve fireworks

Our friends Karen and Barry went back to their home in Geneva for Christmas and returned in late December, and we were invited to their house for New

Year's Eve dinner. The New Year's Eve fireworks in Funchal are world famous, and we had a ringside view from the balcony of their house, perched on a hillside with views over the harbour.

Moving down the mountain

Where we were living in Palheiro was on the edge of the cloud belt, which meant our apartment could be enveloped in misty cloud while it remained sunny down at sea level in Funchal. In early December we made the decision to give notice and to find somewhere closer to the sea and the centre of Funchal. I was lucky enough to find a lovely small typical Madeiran house in a cul-de-sac close to the bus and within walking distance of town.

Rue Lazaretto

On 1 February 2021 we moved to 31 Rue Lazaretto, which was our home until we returned to Ireland on 6 June. We thought it important that our neighbours knew we were not typical holidaymakers but that we would be living there for six months. Using Google translate I introduced ourselves. A local copy shop printed some postcards for me, and I dropped them into the neighbours' letter boxes. No more than an hour later, our gate bell rang and we were greeted by one of the neighbours, Rita, who came with a basket of vegetables and a note in English written by her daughter, welcoming us.

Because of language challenges we never got past 'bom dia' and 'thank you' but that didn't seem to matter. Mid-morning toot-tooting announced the arrival of the bread man's van; he stopped in our lane and we'd join the neighbours, who gathered around the van to buy fresh bread.

The first few times we walked up our lane, our passing would cause a cacophony of dog barking. However, after a week or so, we could walk past gateways and be greeted by tails wagging or indifference.

Saint Patrick's Day

We decided to celebrate Saint Patrick's Day, and Jackie thought it would be nice to bake cupcakes and decorate them with green icing. We spent a morning scouring Funchal for green icing but with no success. I eventually found coloured icing on Amazon. I handed over an obscene amount of money, and about a week later the icing arrived from Germany.

The Birdman of Madeira

I designed a Saint Patrick's Day card with an appropriate greeting in Portuguese and I had twenty printed. We bought small gift bags and put a green cupcake and Saint Patrick's Day card into each and delivered them to our neighbours. The tricolour was hung on our little patio and the sun shone – a Paddy's Day to remember.

Swimming

From our little house we were able to walk down to nearby Barreirinha Lido to swim and sunbathe. During the spring the complex was open, but Jackie and I were often the only patrons. Madeira has no real beaches, so we had to walk down steps or a ladder and launch ourselves into deep water. During our swim one of the lifeguards would keep a discreet watch over us.

Meanwhile in Dublin

Back in Dublin our daughter Elaine and her husband, Felim, had made an offer to purchase a house, but closing the sale was a long, drawn-out process, which resulted in us staying on in Madeira for an extra month, which was no great hardship.

Vaccination

Our priority was to get vaccinated before returning to Ireland. Our first step was to get a Certificate of Residency and a Health Number, without which we couldn't get vaccinated. While everyone we interacted with was very helpful, it took time and patience to navigate the bureaucracy. We made what seemed like endless visits to the fifth floor of the Bom Jesus clinic in Funchal. Finally, on one visit we heard the twirling of a laser printer and the magical sound of two certificates being printed and stamped – we finally had our Health Numbers.

In early April we were offered an appointment to get our Covid vaccinations. It was very well organised. We were registered, and I was given a booth number, where a nurse was waiting. However, Jackie's name was not on the list because it was only for over-seventies that day. The receptionist kindly arranged for us to come back a couple of days later, and we were both vaccinated.

Living on the southside
Shortly before we were due to return to Ireland, we received unwelcome news from Elaine; the closing date for her new home was delayed, and even more bleak was a warning from their solicitor that the purchase might collapse completely. We made the decision that Elaine and family would remain in our house, and we'd rent in Dublin for a couple of months until the situation was resolved. I soon discovered that finding a furnished apartment on a short-term lease was next to impossible and/or very expensive.

Out of the blue a colleague from my USIT days, Marie Stack, kindly offered us the use of a three-bedroom townhouse in Rathgar, a posh suburb on the southside. Marie and her husband, Sean, had moved to Kerry but kept the house as an investment and for use by family and friends on trips to Dublin. We arrived back in early June 2021, and after ten days quarantine we were free to enjoy the lovely walks along the River Dodder and the convenience of the Number 14 bus stop almost on our doorstep.

The Doomsday situation didn't arise, and Elaine and family moved into their new home on 6 July, and we were back in Grosvenor Court the following day.

We were truly blessed to have met wonderful, generous people during our eight-month adventure in Madeira and Rathgar. It was a win-win situation: Elaine and family looked after our house, saved a few bob and got a super home, and we missed the worst of the winter weather and lockdowns, enjoyed our life on Madeira, got vaccinated and didn't get Covid.

Where to next?

Printed in Great Britain
by Amazon